KING ARTHUR

DARK AGE WARRIOR AND MYTHIC HERO

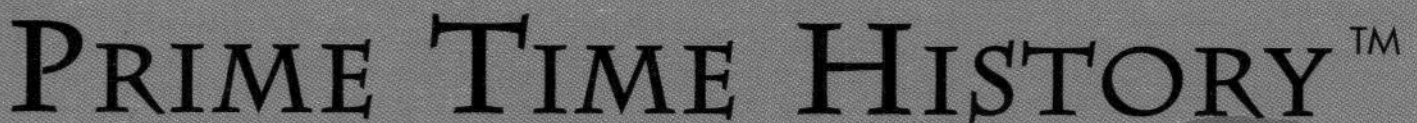

Prime Time History™

John Matthews

King Arthur

Dark Age Warrior and Mythic Hero

Rosen Publishing®
New York

North American edition first published in 2008 by:

The Rosen Publishing Group, Inc.
29 E. 21st Street
New York, NY 10010

Art Editors: Vicky Holmes and Adam Wright
Design: Zöe Mercer
Project Editor: Amie McKee
Editorial: Sarah Larter
Picture Research: Steve Behan
Production: Lisa Moore

Library of Congress Cataloging-in-Publication Data

Matthews, John.
King Arthur: Dark Age Warrior and Mythic Hero (Prime Time History)
p. cm.
Includes index.
ISBN-13: 978-1-4042-1364-7 (library binding)
1. Arthur, King—In literature. 2. Arthurian romances—History and criticism. 3. Arthur, King. I. Title.

PN57.A65M38 2008
809'.93351—dc22

2007033533

Manufactured in the United States of America

Photo Credits

The publishers would like to thank the following sources for their kind permission to reproduce the pictures in the book.

AKG London: 47; /Erich Lessing 26, 88

Album Archivo Fotografico: Orion/Warner Brothers/Cortesia Album: 32; /M.G.M./Cortesia Album: 112

Anne Marie Ferguson: 62

Bill Cooper: 111tr

Birmingham Museum & Art Gallery: Joseph Gaskin: 33

The Bridgeman Art Library: Astley-Cheetham Art Gallery, Stalybridge: 88r; /Bibliotheque Nationale, Paris; 10, 39, 45, 58, 65, 80, 96; /British Library, London, UK: 34; /Christie's Images: 66; /Giraudon: 29; /John Rylands University library, Manchester: 18; /Lambeth Palce Librar, London, UK: 44; /Prado, Madrid, Spain: 93tl; /Private Collection: 35, 95; /Victoria & Albert Museum, London: 42

British Council: DACS/Trustees of the David Jones estate: 8

British Library: 17

Corbis Images: 51; /Archivo Icongrafico, S.A.: 79, 91tl, 106; /Bettmann: 59, 83, 91br, 104; /Burstein Collection: 100, 101; /Charles & Josette Lenars: 60-61; /Christie's Images: 71, 99; /Francis G. Mayer: 6, 9, 31, 46, 87; /Hulton-Deutsch Collection: 108; /Stapleton Collection: 69

John Matthews: 84

King Arthur's Great Halls: 68; /The Sword in the Stone Ltd.: 97; /William Hatherell: 38

Leicester Galleries: Peter Nahum at The Leicester Galleries, www.leicestergalleries.com: 20

Mary Evans Picture Library: 23, 70, 76, 89; /Arthur Rackham: 20

Meg Falconer: 74
Michael J. Stead: 12-13, 21, 22, 24-25. 43, 49, 50, 52, 80, 90, 93, 94, 98tr, 98tl

Miranda Gray: 30

Paisley Museum & Art Galleries: John Duncan: 40

Paul Bonner: 75

Picture-Desk: Art Archive/Tate Gallery/Elleen Tweedy: 37; /Art Archive/Biblioteca Nazionale Turin: 86; /Art Archive/Biblioteca Nazionale, Turin: 54, 57; /The Kobal Collection/Lucas Film/20th Century Fox: 114; /The Kobal Collection/TNT/WB/Holtz: 102; /The Kobal Collection/Warner Bros: 113

Rex Features: The Everett Collection: 115

Ronald Grant Archive: 56

RWCC:111tl

Stuart Littlejohn: 73

Yvonne Gilbert: 28, 77, 92

Every effort has been made to acknowledge correctly and contact the source and/or copyright holder of each picture, and Carlton Books Limited apologizes for any unintentional errors or omissions, which will be corrected in future editions of this book.

CONTENTS PAGE

INTRODUCTION

ARTHUR: MAN OR MYTH

Before Arthur was born Merlin, who was a great prophet, foretold that a king should come of Uther Pendragon; and that storytellers would make a table of this king's breast, and that excellent poets would sit there, and eat their fill before they departed; and wine-draughts draw from this king's tongue; and drink and revel day and night because of him; and that this game should last them to the ending of the world.

LAYAMON—THE BRUT

OPPOSITE: This detail from a fourteenth-century Flemish tapestry depicts Arthur as a great medieval king.

THE WORDS ON THE preceding page, written by the Anglo-Saxon author Layamon in the eleventh century, are astonishingly prescient. Since the appearance of a British, or possibly Romano-British, warrior bearing the name Arthur, sometime in the sixth century, poets and writers of virtually every persuasion have been telling and retelling his story. In the process they have created a rich and heady brew that continues to inspire and entertain people worldwide to this day.

Among the legion of scholars who have studied the evidence for Arthur's existence there has been little agreement. Some have maintained that he is purely fictional, the product of political and nationalistic longings for a golden age that never existed. Others, carefully sifting the scattered fragments of material, found in a handful of documents that chronicle the so-called "Dark Ages," have detected a shadowy form that might, just possibly, be Arthur. But what kind of an Arthur? Certainly not the medieval king in shining armor that most of us know from the stories of our childhood or glamorous Hollywood movies. But if not this Arthur, then who—or what—was he? Was he a man or a myth?

The truth is that Arthur was almost certainly both. It is not entirely possible to unravel the strands of myth, legend and history that have contributed to the creation of his character, so closely are these woven. It is not even certain which came first—because a sixth-century leader called Arthur, who may be seen as the catalyst for much of the story that followed, almost certainly absorbed elements of a more ancient, mythic hero with the same, or a similar name. Within a few years of the departure from the scene of this charismatic figure, further layers of mythic association began to gather around him, enshrining his actual deeds forever in a timeless garment of legend, but disguising the true nature of the man, if he existed, from all but the most dedicated scrutiny.

So, it is not enough to describe Arthur as a Romano-British general—though this he almost certainly was—any more than it will do to call him a figure of myth and legend. When we think about Arthur we really have to have two pictures in mind. One shows a grim sixth-century soldier, named the "Red Ravager" by Christian monks from his own time, accompanied by a ragtag band of men dressed in a hodgepodge of armor from several periods. The second image is of a noble kingly hero of medieval romance, clad in shining mail and wielding the magical sword, Excalibur. In this book we will be tracing both aspects of the picture, looking at where they overlap, how the one influenced the other, and how the mythic underlay of Celtic Britain had a great deal to do with the way both the man and the myth are remembered today.

In addition we will also chart the way in which other themes became attached to the central story of Arthur, exploring how the story of the Round Table came into being and drew into its sphere of influence stories of heroes such as Lancelot, Gawain and Perceval. The result of these embellishments was to make the Arthurian saga one of the most popular legends in the Western world.

So popular, indeed, did these stories become during the Middle Ages, that actual fights sprang up between those who believed implicitly in Arthur, and those who sought to cast doubt on his existence. One medieval writer, Herman of Tournai, described how a traveler visiting Brittany happened to remark that the stories of Arthur were lies. He was immediately attacked and only narrowly escaped with his life. Toward the end of the twelfth century, another writer, Alanus de Insulis, was able to say:

> *What place is there within the bounds of the empire of Christendom to which the winged praise of Arthur the Briton has not extended? Who is there, I ask, who does not speak of Arthur the Briton, since he is but little less known to the peoples of Asia than to the Bretons, as we are informed by our palmers who return from the countries of the East?*

As Arthur's fame spread, yet more traditions became part of the expanding saga. The quest for the Holy Grail, that most mysterious of sacred relics, became a central goal of the Fellowship of the Round Table, inspiring one of the greatest and most enduring legacies of world literature and spirituality. Ancient themes from the earliest history of humankind were recovered and inserted in to the inexhaustible cauldron of the story. Fairytale and vision, prophecy and magic were the common coin of the medieval storytellers who took fragments of folklore, myth, and legend and spun from them the pure gold of the Arthurian saga.

In more recent times, writers as diverse as Thomas Hardy, T. S. Eliot, Mark Twain, and John Steinbeck have found inspiration in the stories of Arthur; while a legion of less well-known authors continue to pour forth a veritable flood of Arthurian novels, plays, poems and movie scripts. A decade of Pre-Raphaelite painters took Arthurian themes as their subject during the Victorian era, and in our own time painters as diverse as the Anglo-Welsh artist David Jones and the Russian Nicholas Roerich have kept the theme alive in the world of art.

The modern medium of the cinema has not been slow to take up the subject of Arthur. Movies such as John Boorman's *Excalibur* (1981), Terry Gilliam's *The Fisher King* (1991) and Jerry Zucker's *First Knight* (1995) have all added their touch of Arthurian magic in recent years. As I write, a new movie based on the story of Tristan and Iseult is in production, while two other filmed interpretations of the Arthurian story are set to appear on our television screens in 2004. The most exciting addition to the movie versions is the forthcoming Jerry Bruckheimer production *King Arthur* (2004). This Dark Age story, written for the screen by David Franzoni (of *Gladiator* fame) and directed by Antoine Fuqua, traces an unusual association between Sarmatian warriors from the Steppes of Russia, imported into Britain with the Roman legions, who brought with them myths and stories from their own lands and influenced the shaping of the Arthurian saga.

Whichever of these new visions of the Arthur legend will succeed in catching the imagination of the public remains to be seen; but whatever the outcome, one thing is certain—interest in the stories of Arthur and his heroes shows no sign of abating. It is more than likely that in another hundred years people will still be asking for tales of Arthur, just as they did within years of his departure from the stage of history. What form those stories will take we cannot say—only that they will almost certainly continue to revolve around the age-old themes of love, heroism, adventure, and the striving to make something better of ourselves.

John Matthews, Oxford, 2003

The Lord of Venedotia, by the twentieth-century artist David Jones, represents Arthur as a Dark-Age chieftain.

1 THE HERO

OPPOSITE: This fifteenth-century illumination shows the medieval hero King Arthur anachronistically fighting the Roman emperor Lucius.

Arthur of far-flung fame,
Bear of the Host, giver of shelter ...
Arthur of the terrible sword
Your enemies fall before you.

ANON: ARTHUR AND THE EAGLE

An Age of Darkness

Heroes come into being for a number of reasons. Sometimes it is to put right a wrong, sometimes to institute a profound change in society, sometimes to bring back treasure, both of this world and the other. The hero whom we know as Arthur came into being in answer to a cry for help from a people in crisis.

At the beginning of the fifth century CE, the once-mighty empire of Rome was beginning to crumble. It would last for another few hundred years, but would never return to its former glory, when it had stretched from Africa in the south to Scotland in the north, from Spain in the west to Armenia in the east. Rome's borders were now shrinking back upon themselves, and the occupying legions had begun to withdraw from outlying provinces, summoned home to protect the Eternal City itself.

As the year 410 CE came to an end in one of these provinces, the island of Britain, the mists drew back behind the last departing Roman galley, and the ancient land was once again returned to its previous masters—the Celts. Indeed, this fierce and independent people had never been truly subjugated, and many areas of Britain had remained free of Roman influence, creating a criss-cross of opposing factions across the entire island.

Nor was the withdrawal of the legions all that sudden. As the historian Nora Chadwick remarked in her book *The Celtic Realms*: "The Roman occupation of Britain can best be likened to a great flood tide, and the close came as the tide recedes, not by a sudden event, not even by a series of sudden events, but by a gradual process, as the ebb-tide leaves the shore." Thus in 407 CE, Constantine, the governor of the province, had been persuaded, somewhat against his will, by the remaining legions in Britain to assume the title of Emperor and to lead an ill-fated exodus to Gaul. There, he perished in battle against overwhelming forces, though his name was remembered in Britain and we shall meet him again in a different guise later on in this book. From this point onward, as the Byzantine historian Procopius later declared, "the Romans were never able to reconquer Britain, which continued to be governed by tyrants."

However, nearly five centuries of Roman occupation had wrought enormous changes across the country, especially in the south and west, where the greatest concentration of Roman power had been sited. The original network of native roads had

Left: The romantic splendor of Tintagel Castle in Cornwall, which has long been held to be the birthplace of Arthur.

been extended and improved, allowing greater freedom of travel and a wider system of commerce. The old scattering of tribal centers had been partially replaced by towns and cities, largely self-governing after the manner of other Roman provinces. In addition, many of the legionaries who had served in Britain chose to remain behind, having fallen in love with the soft hills and deep woodlands of the landscape. Some had married native women and fathered families. Others had been granted tracts of land as payment for their military service and now scraped a living as farmers. Even some of the leading families of the native tribes had adopted Roman ways and were occasionally more Roman than their masters. A determined Romano-British aristocracy clung to its centers of power and tried to weld the tattered remnants of the Roman province into what it had once been.

Tyrants and Saviours

Opposing this last vestige of Roman influence were a number of tribal leaders, the "tyrants" mentioned by Procopius—petty kings ruling over a few hundred acres of land, raiding across the borders of their neighbors as they had done before the coming of the legions. Each one saw himself as a potential High King, wielding supreme power in the land and receiving fealty from lesser lords. Some of their names have survived amid the broken littoral of those dark days: Cunomaglus, Vortiporix, Cradlemas—and a greedy and ambitious man whose name has come down to us as Vortigern, though that name may be nothing more than a title, meaning "great lord." Having won many of the tribal leaders to his cause, promising that the legacy of Rome would be purged forever from the earth of Britain, by 425 CE he had declared himself High King over all Britain. Clearly no lover of things Roman, Vortigern saw to it that by 450 CE most of the last vestiges of the old imperial system of government had almost completely broken down, leaving Britain in a confused and shaky state.

During this time enemies, old and new, appeared to harass the Britons. Picts and Scots from the north and Irish from across the sea to the west began, as they had before the coming of the Romans, raiding ever deeper into the heartlands of the country. Without the presence of the Roman legions there was little to prevent their arrival; and a new scourge, the Saxons, Angles and Fresians from the northwest of Europe, began raiding all along the southern and eastern coasts of Britain. To Vortigern is attributed the idea of setting one enemy against the other, by offering lands to the Saxons in return for help in driving out the Picts and the Irish.

Three sources speak of this time, none judged reliable in all cases, and occasionally contradicting each other. However, from a careful reading of all three, we can get at least a glimpse of the events that took place in war-torn Britain. The first source, and by far the most detailed, is a work known as *De Excidio et Conquestu Britanniae* (*The Fall and Conquest of Britain*) attributed to a monk named Gildas, who probably lived no more than fifty years after the events he was describing. The text is really more of a diatribe against evil and tyrannical leaders—including Vortigern—whom Gildas saw as seeking to restore the old pagan ways of the land and to outlaw the recently established religion of Christianity.

Gildas's account of what happened after Vortigern came to power is laced with invective and worth quoting in full:

> *Then all the counselors, together with the proud tyrant Gurthigern [Vortigern], the British king, were so blinded that, as a protection to their country, they sealed its doom by inviting in among them (like wolves into the sheep fold) the fierce and impious Saxons, a race hateful both to God and men, to repel the invasions of the northern nations [i.e. the Picts, Scots, and Irish]. Nothing was ever so pernicious to our country, nothing was ever so unlucky. What palpable darkness must have enveloped their minds—darkness desperate and cruel! Those very people whom, when absent, they dreaded more than death itself, were invited to reside, as one may say, under the selfsame roof . . . A multitude of whelps came forth from the lair of this barbaric lioness, in three cyuls, as they call them—that is, in three ships of war, with their sails wafted by the wind and with omens and prophecies favorable, for it was foretold by a certain soothsayer among them, that they should occupy the country to which they were sailing three hundred years, and a half of that time, a hundred and fifty years, should plunder and despoil the same.*

There is no reason to doubt Gildas's account, despite its exaggerated tone, at least in its essential details. Britain was essentially undefended at this time—rich and easy pickings for the land-hungry adventurers from the north.

The second of the three sources, the *Historia Brittonum* (*History of Britain*) is attributed to Nennius, another monk. It differs slightly from Gildas, while following the same basic pattern of events. Nennius, who probably lived toward the end of the seventh century, is somewhat more fanciful; he is making, in his own words "a heap of all he can find," drawing on aural reports, fragmentary writings and still-living traditions to make an impressionistic history of Britain.

For years the Britons lived in fear. Vortigern was king ... and during his reign he was threatened both by the Picts and Scots ... then three boatloads of men, banished from Germany, arrived. Among them were the brothers Hengist and Horsa, the son of Guietgils, the son of Guitta, the son of Wodin ... the son of Geta, which made him son of God, not the God of Gods, amen, the God of armies, but one of the idols they worshipped. Vortigern welcomed them and gave them the island they called Thanet, which the Britons call Rudhim ...

Once again Vortigern is the villain responsible for making the Saxons welcome, though here they are represented as exiled men, presumably driven out for some unspecified crime. The Saxon leaders, Hengist and Horsa, are described as descended from the God Wodin, a detail that chimes well with historical fact, as the Saxons often claimed descent from the gods to endorse their fame and status.

The third and final source for this period comes from *The History of the English Church and People* by the Venerable Bede, generally considered one of the most sober and accurate records of Dark Age history. We have no precise record of his source for this period, although he appears to have been familiar with both Nennius and Gildas. Writing *c.*731, his account reads as follows:

In the year of our Lord 449 ... the Angles and Saxons came to Britain at the invitation of King Vortigern in three longships and were granted lands in the eastern part of the island on condition that they protected the country: nevertheless their real intention was to attack it. At first they engaged the enemy advancing from the north and having defeated them, sent back news of their success to their homeland, adding that the country was fertile and the Britons cowardly. Whereupon a larger fleet came over with a great body of warriors, which, when joined to the original forces, constituted an invincible army. These also received grants of land and money from the Britons, on condition that they maintained the peace and security of the island against all enemies. ... These newcomers were from the three most formidable races of Germany, the Saxons, Angles, and Jutes ...

All three accounts agree on certain points. The first Saxons arrived in three boats, began raiding inland and were bought off with a gift of land and a request to help the Britons protect themselves against the Picts and the Irish. The idea of making one's potential enemies into allies was hardly a new one. It had worked before and it would work again. But the Britons seem not to have realized where it would lead.

The Long Knives

At first all went well. The Saxon warriors fought off repeated attacks by the Picts, and helped consolidate a front line along the old Antonine Wall built by the Romans across the neck of land between present-day Carriden, near Edinburgh, and Old Kilpatrick, northwest of Glasgow on the River Clyde. However, soon more and more Saxons began to arrive in Britain, supposedly to help the Britons but in actual fact hungry for lands and plunder. Nennius tells how at this time Vortigern fell for the charms of Hengist's daughter, Rowena, whom he is said to have married. He was then persuaded to grant even larger areas of land to his erstwhile family. Bede, taking the opportunity to attribute the causes for what followed to the "sins" of the Britons, tells us what happened next:

It was not long before such hordes of these alien peoples crowded into the island that the natives who had invited them began to live in terror, for the Angles suddenly made an alliance with the Picts whom they had recently repelled, and prepared to turn their armies against their allies. They began by demanding a greater supply of provisions; then, seeking to provoke a quarrel, threatened that unless larger supplies were forthcoming, they would terminate their treaty and ravage the whole island ... In short, the fires kindled by the pagans proved to be God's just punishment on the sins of the nation ... these heathen conquerors devastated the surrounding cities and countryside, extended the conflagration from the eastern to the western shores without opposition, and established a stranglehold over nearly all the doomed island.

Bede goes on to paint a grim picture of cities burned to the ground, priests killed at their altars, wide-scale famine and death, people sold into slavery and whole communities put to the sword. Vortigern's standing, not surprisingly, diminished rapidly from here on, and he became a fugitive from his own people. His son, Vortimer (Guothermyr) briefly took over his father's role and, being a far more sympathetic figure, succeeded in raising an army to fight back against the Saxons. Indeed, he was so successful that he won several major victories against his father's former allies. Then Vortimer died suddenly—supposedly poisoned by a Saxon spy.

This brief reversal of fortune was sufficient to put Vortigern back into favor for sufficient time to enable him to attempt a conciliatory meeting with the Saxon leaders, Hengist and Horsa. He arranged a gathering between his own chieftains, as many of the British leaders who were still prepared to listen to him, and the Saxons. What followed is vividly described by Nennius:

The enemy planned to overcome Vortigern and his army by cunning … [Both] the Britons and the Saxons were to come unarmed to solemnly swear an alliance. But Hengist ordered his men to hide their knives [in their boots]. "And when I say Eu Saxones eniminit saxas, *take your knives out of your boots and attack them. But do not kill their king. For the sake of my daughter, his wife, take him prisoner because he will be more use to us as a hostage for ransom." They promised to obey and went to the meeting. The Saxons spoke like friends and behaved with great courtesy. The men sat down so that each Saxon sat next to a Briton. Then Hengist cried out as he had said he would and the three hundred chiefs of Vortigern were all slaughtered. He alone was taken prisoner and put in chains. To save his life and win his freedom he had to cede many regions, including Essex, Sussex and Middlesex.*

This iniquitous event, afterward known as the Night of the Long Knives, ended any support or respect for Vortigern. He became a hunted man again, with virtually every hand against him. He fled to Wales, where a few of his original followers still remained faithful, and was followed there, according to Nennius, by Saint Germanus, whom some authorities describe as his son by his own sister. Whatever the truth of this, Germanus had carried out a furious campaign to discredit Vortigern and damn him still further in the eyes of the people. The end of the story is told by Nennius:

Vortigern fled in shame to … the land of the Demetae near the river Tiebi. Saint Germanus followed him there also, and remained for three days and nights, fasting with his clerics. On the fourth night the whole fortress was set alight by fire from heaven … and Vortigern perished together with all his companions … Others again say that the earth opened and swallowed him up the night his fortress burnt around him, for after the fire nothing of him or his companions could be found.

Another, far more racy, account of these events was to reappear in a much later text which, as we shall see in chapter three, introduced an eternally enduring figure into the story.

A Flame in the Darkness

Power in Britain now passed into the hands of a coalition of lords under the leadership of one Ambrosius Aurelianus, who was referred to as "The Last of the Romans." It is clear from this name that he represented the faction who desired a return to Roman ways or was in fact of Roman ancestry. One source even mentions his "royal" parents, suggesting that he may have sprung from a marriage between one of the old noble families of Britain and a high-ranking Roman official.

Ambrosius sought, and succeeded to some degree, in keeping the spirit of Roman civilization alive. He seems to have maintained a permanent military force, drawn from more than one tribe, to have kept the Roman roads open, and to have offered some kind of defense for the families and farmers who wanted only to pursue their lives in peace. He offered support and strength to the crumbling civil administration, which somehow continued to function, if fitfully, for almost fifty more years.

After Vortigern's reign of cruelty and betrayal, Ambrosius must have seemed like a veritable saviour. Under his leadership the Saxons were pinned down along the coastal regions and trade with the continent was re-established. Oil, wine and a type of luxury pottery called "samian" were imported into the country by wealthy Britons. Sources in general imply that peace returned in some measure to the land at this time. As Bede puts it:

The Britons slowly began to take heart and recover their strength, emerging from the dens where they had hidden themselves, and joining in prayer that God might help them to avoid complete extermination. Their leader at this time was Ambrosius Aurelius, a modest man of Roman origin, who was the sole survivor of the catastrophe in which his royal parents had perished. Under his leadership the Britons took up arms, challenged their conquerors to battle, and with God's help inflicted … defeat upon them. Thence forward, victory swung first to one side, and then to the other, until the battle of Badon Hill, when the Britons made a considerable slaughter of the invaders …

Mention of this battle is crucial, for it signals the appearance of a new hero, one whose star was to rise rapidly to the ascendant and has remained there, almost unopposed, ever since. Even with the presence of Ambrosius the new peace was a fragile thing. The Saxons in the south and east and the Picts and Scots in the north threatened the country from three sides; the Britons needed a more virile focus for their newfound independence. One man alone was to provide that focus, and in so doing he not only changed the face of British history, but established himself as one of its greatest and most enduring figures. Though not mentioned by name in Bede's account, it was Arthur, not Ambrosius, who was the victor at Badon.

This fifteenth-century image shows the Battle of Badon, where Arthur finally broke the Saxon army and established peace in Britain for nearly forty years.

Birth of a Hero

In two of the three sources we have been examining there is no mention of Arthur by name—a fact that has prompted some historians of the period to question the existence of Arthur at all. However, though he may not be named, his presence can be inferred. Gildas, whose *De Excidio et Conquestu Britanniae* was written around 540 CE, claims to have been born in the year that the Battle of Badon was fought, which makes him more or less contemporary with the Arthurian period. Bede seems to suggest that Ambrosius was the hero who led the Britons to the crashing victory against the Saxons at Badon, but his wording is vague. It is Nennius who adds significantly to the picture by adding a list of eleven other battles in which the Britons were triumphant and in which Arthur is specifically named.

Bede's interest was more ecclesiastical than military and he may be forgiven for omitting Arthur's name and role. Gildas's silence is more troublesome, especially as he lived so close in

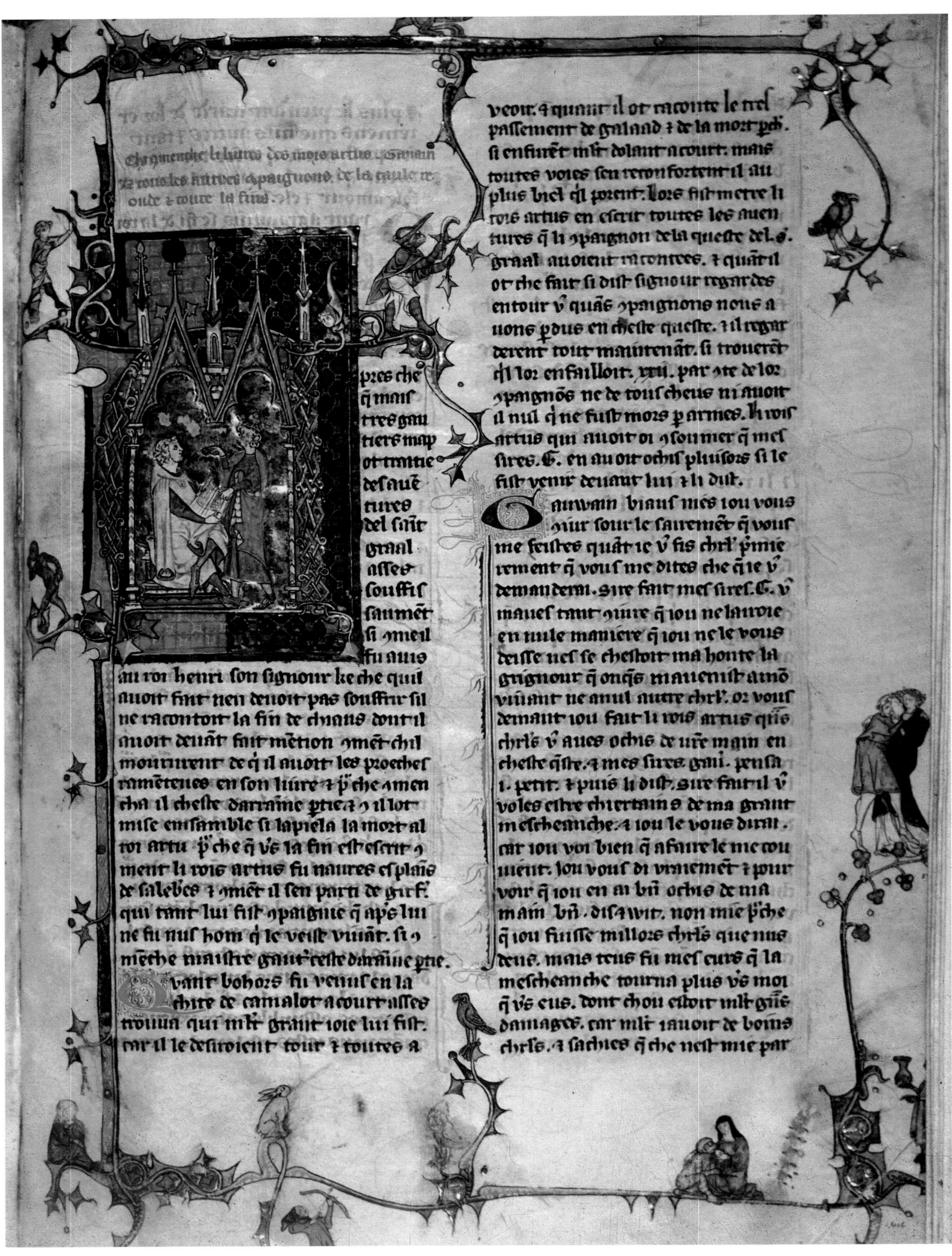

time to the events he describes. But this omission can be accounted for by a tradition that states that he had several brothers, all of whom were pirates, and that Arthur was responsible for their capture and execution. According to one account, when he heard this Gildas took the books in which he had recorded the history of the Arthurian era and, like Shakespeare's Prospero in *The Tempest*, drowned them in the sea.

If we exclude both Gildas and Bede, except for general information, we are left with our old friend Nennius, and an anonymous document known as the *Annales Cambriae* (*Annals of Wales).* An entry for 516 CE in the latter lists "the battle of Badon, in which Arthur bore the cross of our lord Jesus Christ on his shoulders for three nights and the Britons were victorious." This is clear enough in its reference to Arthur, but still does not tell us with any certainty that he was the leader of the Britons. For the essential details we have to turn to Nennius, and to a famous passage in which Arthur's accomplishments are listed in a dramatic way.

> *At that time huge numbers of Saxons were invading Britain and increasing. When Hengist died, his son Octha came from north Britain to the kingdoms of the Canti and founded the royal line of Kent. Then Arthur and the British kings fought the Saxons. He was their dux bellorum [Duke of Battles]. First he fought a battle at the mouth of the River Glein. He fought four others, on the river Dubglas in the region of Linnus. The sixth battle took place on the river called Bassus. The seventh was in the forest of Caledon, the Cat Coit Caledon. The eighth was the battle in the fort of Guinnion, in which Arthur bore the image of the Virgin on his shoulders. The pagans were put to flight that day and many of them were slaughtered, thanks to our lord Jesus Christ and the Blessed Virgin. A ninth battle took place at the City of Legions, a tenth on the banks of the river Tribuit. The eleventh on a mountain called Agned or Cat Bregouin. The twelfth battle took place at Mount Badon, in which a single assault from Arthur killed 960 men and no other took part in this massacre. And in all these battles he was victor.*

This list has given more trouble to would-be chroniclers of the Arthurian period than almost any other. The names are unfamiliar, and their identification cannot be proved beyond a doubt. Nonetheless they establish Arthur as a premier warrior, a *dux bellorum*, making it fairly clear that he was a military leader rather than a king. His royal title comes much later, in the eleventh century, when pseudo-historians and romancers turned Arthur into the mighty, regal figure with which we are still most familiar. The statement that Arthur slew 960 men single-handed has lead many historians to dismiss Nennius's account as spurious—yet this need mean no more than that Arthur's own personal troop led the attack and were supremely successful.

OPPOSITE: A fourteenth-century illumination depicting King Arthur dictating stories of quest and adventure to the scribe Walter Map, who was long believed to be the author of the largest cycle of Arthurian tales.

The Twelve Great Battles

A number of widely divergent theories have been put forward to suggest where these battles were fought and their significance to the history of the period. Carefully studying Nennius's list, the distinguished historian W. G. Collingwood established a coherent pattern of sites that outlines a lengthy campaign in the south, led by a powerful military tactician against the Saxons. Whether this was Arthur or not remains open to question. More recently, Nikolai Tolstoy, who has made a detailed study of all surviving evidence, shifted the sites for the majority of these battles to the north, drawing out the best contemporary guesses from the tangle of conflicting possibilities that may be inferred from Nennius. While Collingwood's theory is not inconsistent with the known facts—such as they are—Tolstoy's findings are more in line with recent thinking.

The first battle took place at a site named Glein, which has been identified as being at or near the River Glen in Northumberland. It was fought against a force of Fresians under the command of Octa, Hengist's son.

The second, third, fourth, and fifth battles were almost certainly fought against Scots from Ulster (Dalraidia). Nennius places them on or close to the River Dubglas in the county of Lindsay. Tolstoy suggests the River Douglas, which is only three miles from the area known as Lennox (Linnius in Latin). Members of the Campbell family in that area claim descent from an Arthur ic Uibar, a possible derivative of Arthur's name, strengthening this supposition.

Battle number six, on the River Bassus, is placed at Cambuslang, also in Scotland. This is long believed to be the burial place of a Pictish chieftain named Caw. Though the name Bassus has not been satisfactorily traced, the name Cambuslang derives from the Latin *camus-long* "the blight of ships," suggesting a possible seafaring engagement. Early genealogies list Caw as the son of the apoplectic Gildas, while his daughter Cwyllog may have been the wife of Medrawt, Arthur's bitterest foe. There are clear references here to a lost story concerning a feud between the families of Caw and Arthur—another possible reason for the omission of Arthur's name from Gildas's work. If Tolstoy is correct in supposing this battle was at sea, it may even have been the one in which the piratical brothers of Gildas met their end.

The seventh battle, at Cat Coit Caledon, has long been recognized as being fought in the areas once occupied by the ancient Caledonian forest. Tolstoy has narrowed this down even further by placing the battle at the meeting place of the borders between the present-day counties of Peebles, Lanark, and Dumfries. A Roman road crosses the mountains here, making an ideal place for a skirmish. The enemy may have been a colony of Saxons from Dumfriesshire.

The eighth battle, at Guinnion, is tentatively identified with Caerguiden (Land's End, in Cornwall) and seems to have been fought against a Saxon leader named Cerdic around the year 500 CE.

The ninth battle, specified as being fought at the City of Legions, proves more difficult to identify, due to the fact that there were several places that bore this name in Arthur's day. Chester is the strongest contender, though Tolstoy prefers Exeter, known by the Romans as Isca Dumnonorium and by the Britons as Caer Wisc. Evidence from a thirteenth-century Welsh poem in the *Black Book of Caermarthen* suggests this was a battle fought either at sea or around a harbor. The hero Geraint, who fell in this battle, was from Devon—making the haven at Exmouth a distinct possibility for the sight of this battle.

The tenth and eleventh battles respectively were possibly fought at the River Tribuit or Tryfrwyd and at Mount Agned, and for these Tolstoy suggests Brent Knoll for the hill, and the nearby area of sands known as either Serts Flats or Berrow Flats, in Somerset for what must have been a long and hard-fought encounter, really a single battle rather than two.

All of these are major battles that would have established Arthur as not only a redoubtable leader, but as the commander of an extremely mobile force, able to move swiftly from place to place, hence the wide distribution of battle sites. Whether or not we accept Collingwood's account of the battle sites, another suggestion made by him carries far more weight. According to this Arthur lead a personal force of mounted *cataphracti*, armored cavalry of the type used both in Rome and Byzantium. This would have given him the mobility and strength to achieve the remarkable reversal of British fortunes that attended his great campaign.

Arthur in the Gruesome Glen by Henry Clarence Whaite shows Arthur setting forth on a solitary adventure—a rare event in the cycles of Arthurian tales.

Ogof Arthur in Anglesey, North Wales. It is believed that Arthur took shelter here during a battle and left treasure in a cave among the rocks.

But it is the twelfth and final battle, cited at Badon, that sees Arthur's star at its zenith. This battle, above all the rest, smashed the Saxon forces and left them so shaken that it was forty years before they dared attack with force again, by which time they were settlers rather than invaders, marrying into British families and establishing a stock that would eventually become a new race—the Anglo-Saxons.

Without Arthur, it is probable that none of this would have happened. The Saxons would have overrun Britain just as the Romans had centuries earlier. As it was, something like a permanent peace was established, which lasted until Arthur's death or disappearance around 545 CE.

Badon itself has been variously identified with Barham Down, Badbury Rings, and Liddington Castle, all in the West Country. The medieval pseudo-historian Geoffrey of Monmouth, who did more than anyone before or since to establish Arthur in the forefront of history, sets it close to Bath in Somerset. Tolstoy, following this, suggests that Bathampton, a hill just outside the present city, fits the bill. He dates the battle as taking place in 501 CE, though the slightly later date of 515 CE seems to fit the meager shreds of information found in Gildas, Nennius and Bede.

The Lost King

This is almost the end of the story of Arthur as it appears in the few surviving historical documents. For its final chapter we must turn to the pages of the tenth-century *Annales Cambriae*, which starkly portray the period in a few enigmatic lines. Under the year 537 CE we find the following entry:

> *The Battle of Camlann, in which Arthur and Medraut fell; and there was death in Britain and Ireland.*

This is all that history has to tell of the passing of one of its greatest heroes. Later, much is made of this in the myth-laden accounts of Arthur's life and deeds. Medraut becomes Mordred, Arthur's bastard son—possibly by his own half-sister, Morgause—and the two become mortal enemies. Here we are only told that both fell, not that they were adversaries, nor related. It is a typical example of the way the fragments of documented fact, eked out with oral tradition, augmented by imagination and the need for a hero of supernatural power, grow with the telling into the vast and wondrous edifice of medieval story.

Beyond these few slight details, history is silent. Ultimately Arthur's true identity remains mysterious.

However, one further source may give us a final clue to the beginning of the legends. It is a theory that takes us back four hundred years before the time of Arthur, to the second century CE, a time when Rome was engaged in ongoing war with a group of wild tribesmen who occupied an area more or less equal in size to modern-day Georgia, in Russia. These people included the Sarmatians, Alans, Izygets, Ossytes, and Scythians, all of whom were impressive warriors and superb horsemen. They were finally defeated by Emperor Marcus Aurelius who, following the practice of stationing foreign troops in Rome's most far-flung outposts, sent some three thousand Sarmatian warriors to Britain. Most were stationed at a fort near the present-day Lancashire town of Ribchester, but some went to garrison the Great Wall built by order of the Emperor Hadrian to keep out the Picts from the far North. Evidence tells us of a Sarmatian contingent garrisoned at the fort of Camboglanna, which, it has been suggested, may have been the site of Arthur's last battle at Camlan, or even the original Camelot. The Sarmatians established a tight-knit community in both locations, and archaeological evidence shows that this was maintained for some time.

The Sarmatians were permitted to keep their own customs, gods, and traditions, including the religious practice of worshipping a sword stuck in a stone. In battle they fought under the leadership of a Roman officer named Lucius Artorius Castus, a seasoned prefect of the VI Vecxtrix Legion who had distinguished himself in campaigns against the Izagetes. The Sarmatian troops also fought under a windsock-style banner, shaped like a dragon and known as the Draco. It was said to roar when they rode into battle. Fierce and proud warriors, they reached an almost legendary status among the Native Britons and were remembered long after this time.

Evidence suggests that their powerful presence, including their beliefs and traditions, influenced the growing saga of the hero Arthur (also known as Artorius) who led a band of mounted warriors, fought under a dragon banner, and proved his superiority by drawing a sword, known as Excalibur, from a stone.

The Iron-Age hill fort of Cadbury Castle in Somerset is widely believed to be a possible site for Camelot, the center for Arthur's Saxon war and later the name of his fabled city.

This woodcut from a sixteenth-century *History of England* shows Arthur engaged with his son Mordred in the Battle of Camlan, where Mordred fell and Arthur was mortally wounded.

Even this weapon, Excalibur, may derive from a Sarmatian source. An older name for it is Caliburn (white-steel), which derives from the words *chalybus* (steel) and *eburnus* (white). Curiously, a tribe of Sarmatian smiths from the area of the Caucasus were known as the Kalybes—suggesting that the very name of Arthur's sword may have originated with the warriors from across the seas.

From these historical facts it is possible to conclude that the presence of the Sarmatians in Britain influenced the creation of the later Arthurian legends, and that Lucius Artorius Castus and his Sarmatian knights may well be the original King Arthur and the Knights of the Round Table. While these facts may be coincidental, all point to a number of historical parallels between the two men.

In the pages of the chroniclers who lived nearest in time to Arthur but were still writing well after the events they describe, he appears and disappears without preamble or comment. He is simply there, does the work allotted to him and then, just as suddenly, vanishes. Winston Churchill wisely remarked in his *A History of the English-Speaking Peoples* that if Arthur did not actually exist, he should have.

Beyond these speculations, and new theories which seem to spring up every few years, lies an unquestionable truth. At the time when Britain faced a plunge into chaos and darkness, a hero emerged who not only succeeded in getting the feuding tribes to work together against their common enemy, but led them in a series of smashing victories that established him as a figure of great power and importance—a figure ripe for developing into the myth-laden king of later accounts.

During the decades that followed his disappearance—no contemporary or near-contemporary account exists of his burial—the Arthur of legend acquired a vast following of warriors, many of whom led lives as colorful and enduring as himself. His legend began to grow almost immediately—as it continues to grow today—gathering ever more extraordinary and amazing details.

Arthur's Quoit on St. David's Head in Wales is one of a number of prehistoric burial chambers that bear the name of Arthur. Though these predate him by thousands of years,

they acted as reminders of his importance in the history of the land.

RE
AR
R

2 THE MYTHIC KING

OPPOSITE: This curious twelfth-century mosaic from the Cathedral of Santa Maria Annunciate at Otranto, Italy, shows Arthur mounted on a goat. The symbolism suggests his connection with the zodiacal sign of Capricorn.

Arthur ran to the cave entrance and threw his knife at the hag, so that it struck her down the center and made her into two vats, and Kaw and Prydyn took the blood and kept it.

CULHWCH AND OLWEN

This contemporary painting by Yvonne Gilbert captures the Dark Age splendor of one of Arthur's warriors, whose armor and weapons reflect the different cultures then present in Britain.

The Second Arthur

Despite the fact that there are so few references to Arthur in either historical or pseudo-historical documents, there is another source that is replete with details and that presents us with a very different and much larger figure. This source is the mythology of the Celts, especially those of Wales and Cornwall. Here we find clues, hints, and stories of rich and extraordinary texture. From these emerges the figure of a second Arthur.

As with all documents relating to myth and legend it is hard to point to a date that might be considered the "earliest" mention of Arthur. This is partly because the references are mostly brief and sometimes were not written down until they had been circulating in oral tradition for several generations. This is the case with a poem attributed to the sixth-century bard Taliesin, a possible contemporary of Arthur's. It may well be the first extant reference not only to the hero of myth but to his quest for a mysterious wonder-working vessel that was later to resurface at the heart of another great strand of the story—the Quest for the Grail.

The *Preiddeu Annwn* or "Spoils of the Inworld" probably dates from the ninth century, some four hundred years after the death of the historical Arthur, yet the references contained within it clearly refer back to a much earlier time—possibly even before the era of Arthur the *dux*. The poem is written in language that is at times obscure and hard to follow, but in essence it tells the story of a voyage, in Arthur's ship *Prydwen*, to the Otherworld kingdom of Annwn, to steal a cauldron possessed of magical properties. We shall examine this text in more detail in chapter six; for now it is sufficient to notice that it places Arthur both in a heroic and mythic milieu, and that his presence in an otherworldly setting is taken for granted.

Elsewhere, in a scattering of poems contained within a thirteenth-century manuscript compilation known as *The Black Book of Carmarthen*, there are references to Arthur that suggest that he was a familiar figure in the repertoire of traditional poets and storytellers. In a poem entitled "The Battle of Llongborth" we read:

At Llongborth I saw Arthur's men
Brave—hewing with steel—
the Emperor's men, the Director of Toil.

This is not the only place where the term Emperor (*Ameradfawr*) is used of Arthur. He appears as such again in several extant poems from this early period. In one such, a series of gnomic verses called "The Stanzas of the Graves," which lists the last resting places of a vast gallery of heroes, we read:

A Grave for March, a grave for Gwythur,
A grave for Gwgawn Red-Sword –
A wonder of the World is Arthur's grave.

The last line is sometimes translated: "Not wise (the thought) a grave for Arthur," which has been taken to refer to the fact that Arthur was believed to be still living and that therefore one should not think of him as having a grave at all. If the first translation is excepted, it probably links Arthur to a number of wondrous graves mentioned elsewhere in Celtic tradition that have strange phenomena associated with them.

Another reference, in a poem again attributed to Taliesin, refers to:

The third profound song of the sage,
Is to praise Arthur, Arthur the blest,
With harmonious art:
Arthur the defender in battle,
The trampler of nine enemies.

The emphasis is on the courage and prowess of Arthur, described as "blest." The historical memory of a great warrior is gradually transformed into one of a mythic hero of even greater stature.

The Bard by John Martin shows a dramatic setting for one of the poets who kept alive the tales of Arthur in the time between his passing and the first medieval romances.

The Porter at the Gate

By far the most interesting of these early poems is a fragment, again found in *The Black Book of Carmarthen*, which is usually given the title "Par Gur?" or "What Man?," taken from its opening line. The poem is given here in full, because not only does it offer a fascinating glimpse into the world of early Welsh epic poetry, it also tells us about the Dark-Age world. It is set in the form of a dialogue between one of Arthur's men and a porter or gatekeeper, whose challenge to those wishing to enter prompts a fusilade of heroic and magical references.

Despite the fragmentary and sometimes oblique nature of this poem (I have completed the last two lines from the sense of what goes before) it gives a powerful sense of the tough, bloody-handed

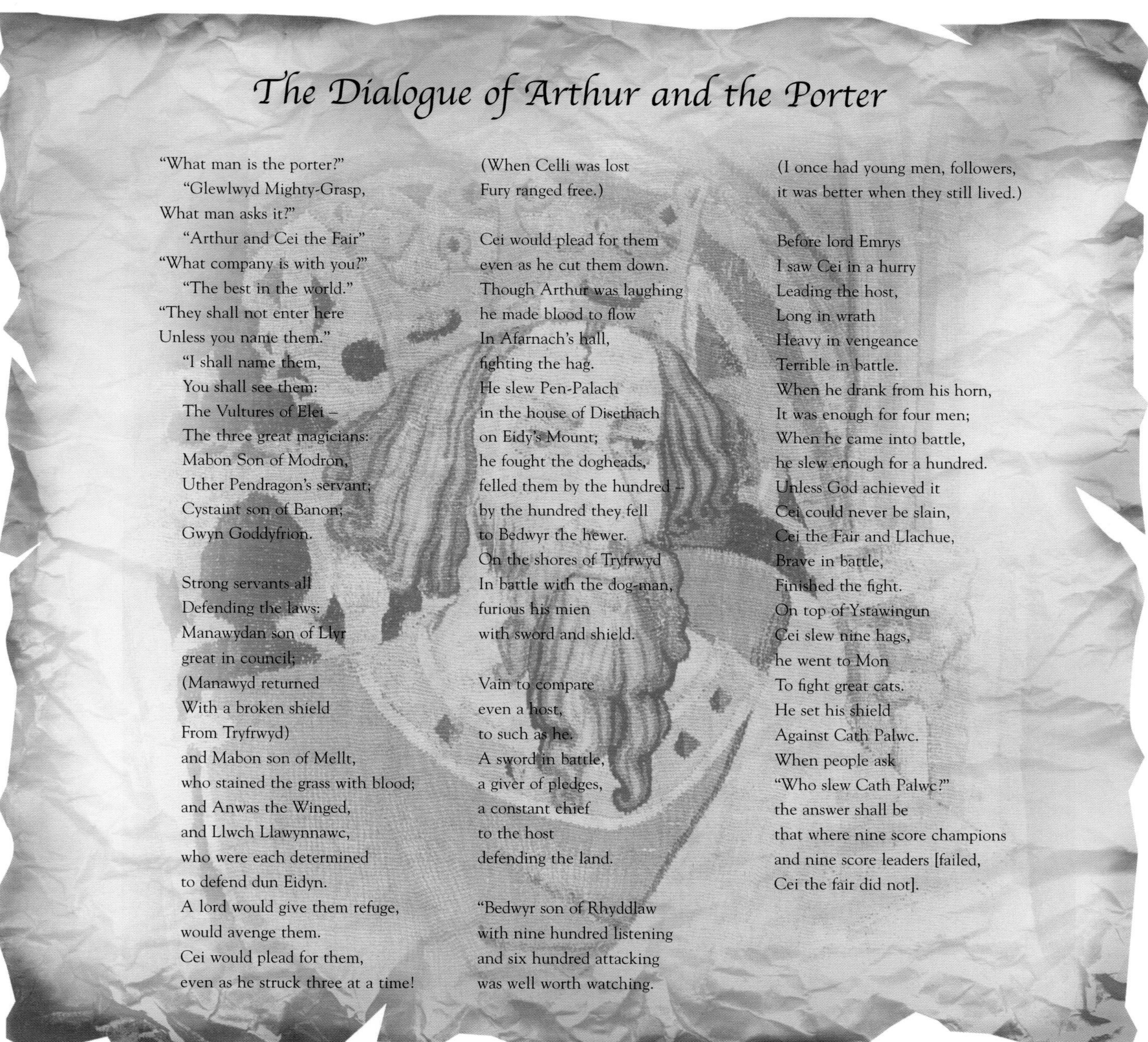

The Dialogue of Arthur and the Porter

"What man is the porter?"
"Glewlwyd Mighty-Grasp,
What man asks it?"
"Arthur and Cei the Fair"
"What company is with you?"
"The best in the world."
"They shall not enter here
Unless you name them."
"I shall name them,
You shall see them:
The Vultures of Elei –
The three great magicians:
Mabon Son of Modron,
Uther Pendragon's servant;
Cystaint son of Banon;
Gwyn Goddyfrion.

Strong servants all
Defending the laws:
Manawydan son of Llyr
great in council;
(Manawyd returned
With a broken shield
From Tryfrwyd)
and Mabon son of Mellt,
who stained the grass with blood;
and Anwas the Winged,
and Llwch Llawynnawc,
who were each determined
to defend dun Eidyn.
A lord would give them refuge,
would avenge them.
Cei would plead for them,
even as he struck three at a time!
(When Celli was lost
Fury ranged free.)

Cei would plead for them
even as he cut them down.
Though Arthur was laughing
he made blood to flow
In Afarnach's hall,
fighting the hag.
He slew Pen-Palach
in the house of Disethach
on Eidy's Mount;
he fought the dogheads,
felled them by the hundred –
by the hundred they fell
to Bedwyr the hewer.
On the shores of Tryfrwyd
In battle with the dog-man,
furious his mien
with sword and shield.

Vain to compare
even a host,
to such as he.
A sword in battle,
a giver of pledges,
a constant chief
to the host
defending the land.

"Bedwyr son of Rhyddlaw
with nine hundred listening
and six hundred attacking
was well worth watching.
(I once had young men, followers,
it was better when they still lived.)

Before lord Emrys
I saw Cei in a hurry
Leading the host,
Long in wrath
Heavy in vengeance
Terrible in battle.
When he drank from his horn,
It was enough for four men;
When he came into battle,
he slew enough for a hundred.
Unless God achieved it
Cei could never be slain,
Cei the Fair and Llachue,
Brave in battle,
Finished the fight.
On top of Ystawingun
Cei slew nine hags,
he went to Mon
To fight great cats.
He set his shield
Against Cath Palwc.
When people ask
"Who slew Cath Palwc?"
the answer shall be
that where nine score champions
and nine score leaders [failed,
Cei the fair did not].

OPPOSITE: An image by Miranda Gray of Arthur's magical ship *Prydwen*, sailing in search of the mysterious Cauldron of Annwn, a pagan vessel that predates the Grail.

Arthur and Guinevere (Nigel Terry, center and Cherie Lunghi, right) depicted in medieval splendor in John Boorman's 1981 movie *Excalibur.*

battlers in Arthur's heroic band. Many of the characters mentioned here are unknown to us from any other source, but some became familiar figures in the later, medieval epics. Thus Cei, who fights the giant Cat Palwc, becomes better known as the acid-tongued blusterer Sir Kay in the later romances. Bedwyr, son of Rhyddlaw, who was "well worth watching" as he single-handedly fought off six hundred foes, becomes Sir Bedivere, Arthur's steward, who is charged with returning the magical sword Excalibur to the lake from whence it came, after Arthur's fatal wounding at the battle of Camlann. Llwch Llawynnawc may well be the original Sir Lancelot.

The Magical Court

All of this gives us an idea of how Arthur and his followers were perceived from the mythic perspective, and within only a few generations of their passing. This is also well illustrated in the stories contained in a collection of Welsh myth and legend known as *The Mabinogion*. Here there are five stories set in and around the Arthurian court. Three of these, "Geraint mab Erbin," "Peredur son of Evrawc" and "Owein," are closely related to the later medieval stories and will be dealt with in chapter four; the others, "Culhwch and Olwen" and "The Dream of Rhonabwy," add further to the Dark-Age myths of Arthur's Britain.

None of the stories contained in *The Mabinogion* were written down until the thirteenth and fourteenth centuries, but the two stories named above contain material that dates from much earlier. Both show signs of being composed no later than the ninth century, and were almost certainly circulating in oral tradition long before that—possibly soon after the end of the actual Arthurian era. "Culhwch and Olwen" tells the story of the trials of a young hero as he attempts to win the hand of Olwen. She is the daughter of the vast and uncouth giant Ysbaddaden Pencawr, who threatens death to all who approach him unless they undergo a series of tests. These include the discovery of several mysterious objects: the Oxen of Glwlwlwyd, the Cup of Llwyr son of Llwyryon, the Hamper of Gwyddno Garanhir, the Harp of Teirtu, the Sword of Wrnach the Giant, and the comb and shears hidden between the ears of the great boar Twrch Trwyth.

In order to achieve this daunting series of quests, Culhwch sets out for the court of Arthur—who is his cousin in this tale—to enlist the aid of various heroes. In fact, not all of the tasks described above are described in the ensuing story, but enough clues are given to suggest a once-substantial cycle of tales, featuring Arthur and his heroes, from which Culhwch and Olwen has been compressed into a single tale. The extent of this epic collection—for the most part lost to us—is suggested by the immense list of the two hundred and fifty heroes that takes up several pages of the text (see Appendix 2, p. 116, for a complete list). Each has a striking or unusual epithet, suggesting their unique skill or ability—for example:

> *Sol, Gwadyn Ossol, and Gwadyn Odyeith (Sol could stand all day upon one foot. Gwadyn Ossol, if he stood upon the top of the highest mountain the world, it would become a level plain under his feet. Gwadyn Odyeith, the soles of his feet emitted sparks of fire when they struck upon things hard, like the heated mass when drawn out of the forge. He cleared the way for Arthur when he came to any blockage.)*

At one time, we may assume, there was a story belonging to each of these individuals. We can only guess at

Kilhwych, the King's Son by Arthur Joseph Glaskin depicts the hero of a tale from the Welsh *Mabinogion*, a twelfth-century collection that preserved many of the oldest stories of Arthur and his warriors.

A fourteenth-century illustration that shows Arthur about to fight with the terrible giant of Mont St. Michel in Brittany. A pig roasts on a spit in the foreground.

the nature of these, but "Culhwch and Olwen" itself gives us a strong impression. The story is not only dramatic and full of magical events, it is also fast paced, funny and contains some of the most richly textured descriptions to be found anywhere in Celtic literature. For example, here is a justly famed description of Culhwch himself, as he first appears, setting out for Arthur's court:

> *And the youth pricked forth upon a steed with head dappled grey, of four winters old, firm of limb, with shell-formed hooves, having a bridle of linked gold on his head, and upon him a saddle of costly gold. And in the youth's hand were two spears of silver, sharp, well-tempered, headed with steel … a gold-hilted sword was upon his thigh, the blade of which was gold … before him were two brindled white-breasted greyhounds, having strong collars of rubies about their necks, reaching from the shoulder to the ear. And the one that was on the left side, bounded across to the right side, and the one of the right to the left, and like to sea-swallows sported about him. And his courser cast up four sods with his four hooves, like four swallows in the air about his head, now above, now below. About him was a four-corner cloth of purple, and an apple of gold was at each corner, and every one of the apples was of the value of an hundred kine. And there was precious gold of the value of three hundred kine upon his shoes and upon his stirrups, from his knee to the tip of his toe. And the blade of grass bent not beneath him, so light was his courser's tread, as he journeyed toward the gate of Arthur's palace.*

If we consider that at one time the bards who traveled the land telling such stories learned all of them by heart, we cannot help but be impressed at the marvelous richness of such descriptive episodes, and the sheer mastery of the detail that decorates the tale.

Culhwch's quest to acquire the miraculous objects demanded by Ysbaddaden becomes an excuse for a riotous assembly of story fragments, woven by a master storyteller into a unique fabric. The centerpiece of the work is the great hunt for the giant boar Twrch Twrch, the end of which is graphically described:

> *And Mabon the son of Modron, came up with him at the Severn … and Arthur fell upon him, together with the champions of Britain; Osla Cyllellvawr drew near and Manawyddan the son of Llyr, and Cacmwri the servant of Arthur, and Gwyngelli, and they seized hold of him, catching him first by his feet, and plunged him in the Severn so that it overwhelmed him. On the one side, Mabon the son of Modron spurred his steed and snatched his razor from him, and Cyledyr Wyllt came up with him on the other side, upon another steed, in the Severn, and took from him the scissors. But before they could obtain the comb, he had regained the ground with his feet and from the moment that he reached the shore, neither dog, nor man, nor horse could overtake him until he came to Cornwall … then Arthur and his hosts proceeded until they overtook the boar in Cornwall, and the trouble that they had met with before was mere play to what they encountered in seeking the comb. But from one difficulty to another, the comb was at length obtained, and then he was hunted from Cornwall, and driven straight forward into the sea. And thenceforth it was never known whither he went …*

In the end of course, with a little help from the fair Olwen herself, who has taken a liking to Culhwch, the tasks are carried out and Ysbaddaden is killed. Culhwch inherits his father-in-law's castle and treasure, and marries his daughter in true fairy-tale tradition. In the process we are treated to an array of wondrous events and adventures, featuring a gallery of Arthurian heroes, all of which makes it plain that Arthur had become the central figure of a far older mythology, taking his place center stage as the prime mover in an already established cycle of native hero-tales.

The Greatest Hero

There are hints of a still older figure, a third Arthur, whom we may call Arth the Bear. Echoes of this being—perhaps even a god in his own right—still come down to us through the pages of the oldest Welsh texts and are hinted at in later folklore references. It may be, indeed, that the Arthur of history subsumed this earlier character, and acquired some of his larger-than-life characteristics. Certainly this is born out in the second of the older stories contained in *The Mabinogion*: "The Dream of Rhonabwy."

This is really a story within a story. Set in the twelfth century it concerns the adventures of Rhonabwy, who may well have been a real person. Fleeing from enemies he takes shelter in the hut of an ancient *gwrach*, or hag. She allows him to sleep on a yellow ox hide, which induces a dream. In this he encounters a huge warrior named Iddawg, who turns out to be one of Arthur's men. He takes Rhonabwy to Arthur's camp, where the warriors are preparing to fight the battle of Badon—which in this case is against the Saxon King, Osla Big-Knife. A series of episodes follow, which Rhonabwy witnesses, including a curious game of *gwyddbwyll* (a game similar to chess). This game, between Arthur and his nephew Owein, is constantly interrupted by messengers, who bring news of a battle taking place in an adjacent field between Arthur's men and Owein's "ravens" (we are not told, but are lead to assume that these may be men who can take the form of ravens or who wear cloaks of ravens' feathers).

Despite this the game continues, so that it becomes a kind of symbolic representation of the actual warfare being fought out nearby. The story goes on:

> *So they finished [one] game and began another; and as they were finishing the game, lo, they heard a great tumult and a clamour of armed men, and a croaking of ravens, and a flapping of wings in the air, as they flung down the armor entire to the ground, and the men and horses piecemeal. Then they saw coming a knight on a lofty-headed piebald horse … and he told him [Arthur] that the Ravens had slain his household and the sons of the chief men of the island, and he besought him to cause Owein to forbid his Ravens. And Arthur besought Owein to forbid them. Then Arthur took the golden chess-men that were upon the board, and crushed them until they became as dust. Then Owein ordered Gwres the son of Rhegwed to lower his banner. So it was lowered, and all was peace.*

RIGHT: A Victorian idea of the great medieval King Arthur painted by Charles Ernest Butler (1864–1918).

Throughout this story Arthur is represented as a figure of god-like proportions. At one point, seeing Rhonabwy, he comments on the "little men" who now occupy Britain, over which he had once ruled. This may be no more than a typical backward glace at a lost, golden age, but it does suggest that by the twelfth century, if not sooner, Arthur was regarded as more-than-mortal, the memory of his life and deeds having taken on a patina that was to outlast the ages.

The Great Queen

As well as the heroes orbiting the figure of Arthur, there are a number of extraordinary women. Most of these will be dealt with in Chapter Five, but one, whose role in the story of Arthur is substantial, must be looked at here. This is Guinevere, Arthur's queen, of whom history is largely silent but who features extensively in the mythic and legendary accounts of the king.

In the later, medieval sources Guinevere is a familiar figure—beautiful but ultimately false to her husband, betraying him with the romantic Lancelot. In the earlier, heroic texts, a somewhat different figure emerges.

There are several mentions of Guinevere in Celtic literature. In the collection known as *The Welsh Triads*, which groups

The Marriage of King Arthur and Queen Guinevere, by John Henry Frederic Bacon. An illustration from a collection of children's stories from Tennyson's *Idylls of the King.*

hundreds of story references in threes and was probably used as a memory-jogger by the bardic storytellers of the early Middle Ages, we find her listed among the unfaithful wives of the Island of Britain:

One was more faithless than those three: Gwenhywfar,
Arthur's wife, since she shamed a better man than any of the others.

Elsewhere in the same collection we hear of not one but three Guineveres:

Three Great Queens of Arthur's court:
Gwenhywfar daughter of Cywryd Gwent,
and Gwenhywfar daughter of Gwythr ap Greidawl,
and Gwenhywfar daughter of Gogfran the Giant.

All these names are obscure, and it is unclear whether any one of the three is to be identified with Arthur's queen. They may even represent a triple-aspected goddess of that name. However, the last of the three named here is remembered in a popular Welsh rhyme, which says: "Gwenhywfar, daughter of Gogfran the Giant—bad when little, worse when big." In later, medieval tradition we are told of two Guineveres, identical sisters, with different mothers but the same father, who are called the "true" and "false" Guinevere, one of whom betrays Arthur, the other becoming a substitute queen while her sister is protected by Lancelot.

But by far the most substantial reference to Guinevere—and probably the earliest—which presents her in a manner closer to the way we know her today, appears in the *Vita Sanctae Gildae* (*Life of Gildas*), a twelfth-century text by the monk Caradoc of Llancarven. In this the irascible author of *De Excidio et Conquestu Britanniae*, whom we encountered in Chapter One, is described in terms we would be hard put to recognize. Here we read how Gildas arrived at Glastonia (Glastonbury) "at the time when King Melwas was reigning in the Summer Country," and was well received. However, at this time, Glastonia

was besieged by the tyrant Arthur with a countless multitude, on account of his wife Gwenhywfar, whom the aforesaid wicked king had violated and carried off, and brought there for protection, owing to the asylum afforded by the invulnerable position due to the fortifications of thickets of reed, river and marsh. The rebellious king had searched for the queen throughout the course of one year, and at last heard that she remained there. Thereupon he roused the armies of the whole of Cornubia and Dibneria; war was prepared between the enemies.

William Morris's *Queen Guinevere* (1858) displays the artist's fascination with the costume and furniture of the Middle Ages.

When he saw this, the abbot of Glastonia, attended by the clergy and Gildas the Wise, stepped in between the contending armies, and in a peaceable manner advised his king, Melwas, to restore the ravished lady. Accordingly, she who was to be restored, was restored in peace and good will.

This has a ring of historical truth about it. Or at least it sounds like a memory of events that may actually have taken place—though it is unlikely, in the light of what we know of Gildas, that he would have taken the trouble to intervene in any matter concerning the "tyrant" Arthur!

The theme of Guinevere's abduction, however, echoes throughout Arthurian literature. It is repeated by Geoffrey of Monmouth in his pseudo-history of Britain, and again in Thomas Malory's *Le Morte d'Arthur*, where Melwas reappears as a knight named Meleagraunce and Guinevere is rescued, not by Arthur, but by Lancelot. In mythological terms, the story is one of several such abduction tales that come under the heading of "the rape of the Flower Bride." This is an ancient theme in which "the sovereignty of the land" is represented by a woman whom the would-be king or ruler must win either in combat against an

Sir Lancelot rescues Queen Guinevere from the stake in this powerful picture by William Hetherall. In the fight that follows, Lancelot accidentally kills his friend Sir Gareth.

adversary or by marriage. In the case of Guinevere, Arthur's marriage to her signifies his partnership with the land; when the queen is stolen away by Melwas he must win her back or lose his crown.

Behind this may well lie the seeds of the whole complex of stories relating to the illicit love of Lancelot and Guinevere. Seen through the eyes of the medieval romancers a tale of adulterous love was a far more interesting story than the pagan story of sovereignty, though it never wholly lost touch with the more ancient theme of the queen's abduction and recovery.

The Dream Behind the Dream

The picture that emerges from these scattered references is a very different one to the later, idealized medieval stories of "King" Arthur and his Knights of the Round Table. It is also different to the glimpses of the actual historical Arthur, the tough battle-leader with his mobile cavalry force, pitted in deadly combat against the Saxons. Here, in the texts dealing with the mythic Arthur, his enemies are monsters like Cath Palwc, or the hag Pen-Palach, or the mysterious "dog-men" mentioned in "Par Gur"? The giant Arthur of "Rhonabwy's Dream" is a distant echo of the historical hero, grown greater in the memory of his people, while ancient themes like that of the King and the Land, are represented by the story of Guinevere and Melwas. In addition, the shadow of a still more ancient figure, Arth the Bear, slips into and out of focus. Is it possible that this god-like being dates back to a period before the coming of the first Celtic people to Britain? As the great Celtic scholar Jean Markale remarks in his book *King Arthur, King of Kings*:

> *The supernatural plays an important part … in all the Arthurian tales. But it is not just a matter of whimsical, fey creatures, rather a desanctified, popular form of ancient religion. The Celtic heroes … are so closely bound up with the divine that it is impossible to tell which of them are gods made men and which men made divine.*

This is true of Arthur, as we have seen. Such echoes of belief almost certainly influenced the Celtic bards who first set the wheels of the Arthurian mythic story in motion, adding detail after detail as they reshaped the figure of the *dux bellorum* into the form of a mighty hero and his warrior companions.

In each case, the figure of the historical Arthur still shines through, but there is a deeper, richer and more archaic style to the mythic king or Emperor. It was from this dream-like figure of myth, legend and history that the mighty king of medieval romance was soon to emerge. Another figure, who accompanied Arthur throughout this transformation, brought in his train a rich heritage of magic and mystery. It is to this character, no lesser person than the great enchanter Merlin, that we must look for the next pieces in the evolving pattern of Arthur's story.

In this fourteenth-century illustration to *The Story of Lancelot*, the Knights of the Round Table are filled with awe by a vision of the Holy Grail.

MERLIN THE WISE

OPPOSITE: *Merlin and the Fairy Queen* by John McKirdy Duncan (1866–1945). Merlin stands face to face with one of the otherworldly women who were to plague his life and ultimately imprison him in a magical tomb.

A lonely man, his head above the stars
Walks on the clean sand white beside the sea –
Merlin, the lonely man of Camelot,
Who left King Arthur and the tournaments ...
To walk beside the waves that curl in foam
And sparking splendor round him.

ANON: ARTHUR AND THE EAGLE

The Welsh Seer

NOWHERE IS THE MYTHIC NATURE of the Arthurian tradition more clearly focused than in the figure of Merlin. Advisor to three kings, prophet, magician, and wise man, Merlin's shadowy presence seldom takes any single form for long enough to observe his real nature. However, he is central to the emerging story of Arthur and plays a hugely important role in the cycles of tales that make up the Arthurian tradition as we know it today. Yet the genesis of this remarkable figure is almost as mysterious and complex as the character of Merlin himself.

Some commentators, including Geoffrey Ashe, view Merlin as a god of the ancient, native people of Britain, his home, at Maridunum (Carmarthen, Wales), the site of his cult. Others, such as Nikolai Tolstoy see in him a shaman or a wildman, while R.J. Stewart views Merlin as a seer whose prophecies are still valid for our own time. Yet Merlin eludes such fixed definitions, his origins and his ultimate fate remain mysterious. Even his own words render him more opaque:

> *Because I am dark, and always shall be, let my book be dark and mysterious in those places where I will not show myself.*

Some aspects of Merlin's career are possible to trace. He first appears, in recognizable form, in the writings of the twelfth-century pseudo-historian Geoffrey of Monmouth, who may have heard stories of Merlin either during his childhood or his later days as Bishop of St. Asaph in North Wales. Either way Merlin plays a considerable role in Geoffrey's *Historia Regum Brittaniae* (*History of the Kings of Britain*) which was written *c.* 1136. He also wrote (or at least compiled) a volume of Merlin's prophecies, which he incorporated into his larger work as part of the history of early Britain.

Opinions as to the veracity of Geoffrey's book have been the cause of scholarly debate for generations, and strongly affect the way that we see Arthur. However, though some critics have dismissed Geoffrey as a flagrant forger, a more recent attitude tends to emphasize his value as a recorder of traditional tales and native folklore. R.J.Stewart, in his valuable study entitled *The Prophetic Vision of Merlin*, has established that Geoffrey must have had access to a large collection of material that recorded the seer's inspired utterances—although whether these were entirely genuine, or represented a Merlin tradition, has yet to be established.

Merlin looks intently at the fairy Nimue, who pretends to ignore him in this painting by Edward Burne Jones (1833–98).

The Falling Tower

Geoffrey recounts the story of Merlin's first dramatic appearance, and of his great prophetic outburst, in colorful language. He begins by telling the story of Vortigern, more or less as it is found in the writings of Nennius and Gildas, which we examined in Chapter One. However, Geoffrey diverges from these accounts, adding details that do not appear elsewhere.

After the Night of the Long Knives, in which the flower of Britain's rulers fell to the weapons of the Saxons, Vortigern flees to Wales, intending to build a stronghold. Having chosen a site he sets his builders to work; but every night the progress they have made is undone by a mysterious agency. Vortigern consults his druids and

Dinas Emrys in North Wales has long been described as the setting for Merlin's famous disclosure of the battling red and white dragons. Emrys is an old Welsh name for Merlin.

learns that only the blood of a fatherless child, spilled on the stones, will ensure the completion of the fortress. Sent out to search for such a child, Vortigern's soldiers discover Merlin at Carmarthen (said by Geoffrey to derive from *Caer Myrddin*, Merlin's Town). He is revealed to be the son of a Welsh princess, but no one knows the origin of his father. The woman and her son are brought before Vortigern, where Merlin's mother explains that she has led a devout and pure life, but that she was visited in her chamber by a shining being who fathered the child upon her.

Vortigern is tempted to disbelieve this account, but Merlin himself speaks out in defense of his mother, and challenges Vortigern and his druids to explain the real reason why the tower will not stand. He tells them that there is a pool beneath the hilltop, within which is a stone coffer containing two dragons, one red and the other white. The dragons battle mightily every night, thus causing the ground to shake and the work of the king's masons to fall. Vortigern orders his men to dig and finds that all is as Merlin had foretold. The wise child then explains that the red dragon symbolizes Britain and the white dragon the Saxons, and predicts that in time the white will overcome the red. He then goes into a trance and for the next 12–14 pages in Geoffrey's book proceeds to expound the future of the British race to the

The fifteenth-century *Chronicle of St. Albans* tells the story of Merlin's revelation of the red and white dragons to the tyrant King Vortigern.

very end of time. In the process he predicts the coming of Arthur "the Boar of Cornwall," which will "bring relief from these invaders, for it will trample their necks beneath its feet," and warns Vortigern of his own forthcoming death. The end of this extraordinary outburst is apocalyptic, with references to a riot among the planetary houses and the fall of deadly rain. Finally,

> *in the twinkling of an eye the seas shall rise up and the arena of the winds shall be opened once again. The winds shall do battle together with a blast of ill omen, making their din reverberate from one constellation to another.*

Merlin's vision of the future is as terrifying as anything foretold by Nostradamus or his ilk. Wherever Geoffrey found the material for this part of his book, it was almost certainly not from his own imagination, indicating, as already stated, that he was in some way the recipient of a body of traditional lore associated with Merlin.

Geoffrey himself claimed that he was merely translating "a certain very ancient book written in the British language," which had been lent to him by Archdeacon Walter of Oxford, and that this was the source of all that he wrote. No trace of this book has ever come to light, and it has often been considered to be an invention of Geoffrey's to add veracity to his fanciful history.

However, there seems no reason to doubt that the book existed, although it is evident that Geoffrey embellished his sources considerably. The source of the story above is Nennius, whom, as we have seen, provides one of the few possibly authentic records of the Arthurian era; however, his youthful prophet was named Ambrosius. It seems that, in order not to confuse him with Ambrosius Aurelianus, who helped overthrow Vortigern, Geoffrey borrowed the name Merlin from an earlier, native figure, Myrddin Wyllt (Merlin the Wild), who may actually have lived either in Scotland or Wales during the sixth or seventh centuries.

This would make Merlin roughly contemporary with Arthur, and it is possible that we have here a genuine tradition of the great war-leader and his inspired advisor, which has been carried through to reappear in Geoffrey's text in a distorted form.

Geoffrey's book became a bestseller in medieval terms, and may well have given the initial impetus to the phenomenon of Arthurian literature. After the episode of Vortigern's tower with his first great prophetic outpouring, Merlin performs several prodigious feats—including transporting a ring of magical stones called "The Giant's Dance" from Ireland to Salisbury Plain, which becomes a vast mausoleum for the kings of Britain. The ring is, of course, known to us as Stonehenge. While Merlin was clearly not responsible for the building of the great megalithic monument, it is possible that even here Geoffrey was recording an ancient tradition relating to the original builders of the great stone circle.

Geoffrey's Merlin serves both Ambrosius Aurelianus and Uther Pendragon, the father of Arthur. It is to Geoffrey again that we owe the story of the hero's conception, in which Merlin magically disguises Uther as the husband of the Duchess of Cornwall so that he can lie with her and beget the future king.

Subsequently Merlin becomes adviser to Arthur, in which guise he is still best remembered, and as which he appears in all the major versions of the story that follow Geoffrey's account. He thus serves three kings, for each of whom he performs remarkable feats, while serving as prophet and counselor. Merlin is never pictured as a mere court magician; there is always something restless and untamable about him, vestiges of a wild and otherworldly dimension continue to cling to him, and for this we owe something to Geoffrey of Monmouth's portrait.

The Life of Merlin

Following on the success of the *Historia*, Geoffrey wrote another book, in Latin verse, which he called *Vita Merlini* (*The Life of Merlin*). In this he extended his account of the famous seer to an even greater degree, painting a very different picture to that of his earlier work. In this version Merlin is a prince in his own right who, driven mad by scenes of carnage at the battle of Arderydd, runs away and lives like a wild beast in the wilderness for many years. On his return to sanity he is recognized as a great prophet and wise man.

Geoffrey was drawing again on the traditions surrounding the mysterious figure of Myrddin Wyllt, who seems to have lived in post-Arthurian Britain, and, like Arthur, appears to have absorbed something of an even earlier, possibly deified being of great antiquity. Some of the writings of the historical Myrddin have actually survived, and show him to have been no mean poet. The poem *Affalannau* (*Apple Trees*), of which a fragment is translated below, speaks of a now forgotten battle between the Cymry (Britons) and the Saeson (Saxons) and locates Myrddin at Celyddon, the Caledonian forest and one of the probable sites of Arthur's seventh battle against the invaders. It also mentions Gewenddolau, a possibly historical prince who lived not long after the time of Arthur.

A fifteenth-century painting from *The Story of Merlin*, showing King Aurelius, his army preparing and Merlin.

Affalannau (Apple Trees)

I

Sweet apple tree, your branches delight me,
Luxuriantly budding, my pride and joy!
I will prophesy before the lord of Macreu,
That on Wednesday, in the valley of Machawy
Blood will flow.
Lloegyr's blades will shine.
But hear, O little pig! on Thursday
The Cymry will rejoice
In their defense of Cyminawd,
Furiously cutting and thrusting.
The Saesons will be slaughtered by our ashen spears,
And their heads used as footballs.
I prophesy the unvarnished truth –
The rising of a child in the secluded South ...

Sweet, yellow, apple tree,
Growing in Tal Ardd,
I predict a battle at Prydyn,
In defense of frontiers.
Seven ships will come
Across a wide lake,
Seven hundred men come to conquer.
Of those who come, only seven will return
According to my prophecy.

Sweet apple tree of luxuriant growth!
I used to find food at its foot,
When, because of a maid,
I slept alone in the woods of Celyddon,
Shield on shoulder, sword on thigh.
Hear, O little pig! listen to to my words,
As sweet as birds that sing on Monday –
When the sovereigns come across the sea,
Blessed be the Cymry, because of their strength.

Sweet apple tree, growing by the river,
Who will thrive on its wondrous fruit?
When my reason was intact
I used to lie at its foot
With a fair wanton maid, of slender form.
Fifty years the plaything of lawless men
I have wandered in gloom among spirits.
After great wealth, and gregarious minstrels,
I have been here so long not even sprites
Can lead me astray.
I never sleep, but tremble at the thought
Of my Lord Gwenddoleu, and my own native people.
Long have I suffered unease and longing –
May I be given freedom in the end ...

(*Translated by the author*)

The poem is full of curious lore and the remains of a tradition that depicts Myrddin living wild among the woods with only a pig, which was regarded as a sacred beast among the Celts, for company. It shows that, whatever else he may have been, Myrddin/Merlin was very much a part of the ancient bardic tradition of Wales. His writings form part of a significant body of literature, which has survived—although not without a good deal of reworking—to the present day. Although it is of a different tone to the accounts of Merlin's later career, many of his magical acts are duplicated in this more primitive strain of material.

By drawing together these elusive traditional threads of tradition Geoffrey provided a foundation on which many generations of writers could build. The wonder-working prophet of *Historia Regum Brittaniae* and *Vita Merlini* proved immensely popular with medieval audiences—as, indeed, he has continued to be. Numerous texts followed that extended Merlin's role even further.

The Devil's Son

Inevitably perhaps, in one so talented in the reading of the stars and the future, Merlin became associated in the medieval consciousness with the idea of necromancy, and thus with the Devil. When the twelfth-century Burgundian writer Robert de Boron set about filling in some of the details of Merlin's history missing from the earlier records (as he had previously done with the Grail legends, *see* Chapter Six), he gave a very different account.

De Boron described the demons of hell, infuriated by Christ's descent and purgation of their overcrowded domain, plotting the birth of an anti-Christ—Merlin. They send forth an incubus to impregnate an innocent princess of Dyfed with an evil child. The plans of the demons are frustrated by the innate goodness of the child's mother, who finds a priest to baptize the infant

An illustration from a thirteenth-century manuscript shows the devil begetting Merlin on an innocent woman.

before evil can take hold of him. The child is born with a hairy pelt and the ability to speak and reason almost from birth. The hair falls from him when he is baptized, but he retains both the power of speech and an otherworldly clairvoyance.

Thus Merlin's abilities are accounted for in terms acceptable to a Christian readership: the "golden stranger" who fathers Merlin in earlier tales becomes a demon; the ancient "god" Merlin becomes a "devil," and powers that would have been wholly appropriate to a Celtic seer become the product of necromancy. The effects remain the same, however—Merlin as magician reigns supreme.

Interestingly, Merlin's mother is described as a princess of Dyfed, and in Geoffrey's *Vita Merlini*, he is also described as a prince in his own right. This seems to add yet another strand to the complex web of associations. No record of a sixth-century noble named either Merlin or Myrddin has come to light, but this does not mean that that the person did not exist. As with Arthur himself, the overlay of mythical and historical figures is so complete that it is no longer possible to differentiate one Merlin from another.

The Prophet and the Wildman

Merlin also assumed some of the attributes and abilities of an even older character: an inspired semi-mythical madman named Lailoken, who hailed from the Lowlands of Scotland at roughly the same period that Merlin may have flourished.

A story common to both men concerns their laughter: in each instance they laugh three times, betraying their uncanny knowledge by so doing. Merlin laughs at the wife of his friend King Rhydderch when he sees a leaf caught in her hair—the heritage of an adulterous tryst. He laughs again at a beggar whom he knows to be sitting over a pot of gold; and a third time at a youth buying a new pair of shoes when in fact he is destined to die within the day. In *Vita Merlini*, Merlin's sister, Ganeida, tests his newly restored sanity, by presenting him with the same youth in three different guises. In each case Merlin predicts a different end for the youth—he will hang, drown and fall to his death. This prediction is fulfilled when the youth falls over a cliff and is suspended by an ankle caught in a tree root with his head beneath the waters of a river.

In the story of mad Lailoken the prophet predicts the threefold death for himself, from which we can infer that the same thing once held good for Merlin. The motif is an extremely ancient one, deriving from the self-initiation, or false-death, of the shaman. The character of Merlin certainly has traces of a shamanic background. His ability to shape-shift at will, his periods of madness, his prophetic and inspired utterances and the motif of the threefold death are all aspects of the shaman's way.

But ultimately Merlin conforms more closely to the idea of the medieval magician. In common with two other early poets, the Celtic Taliesin and the Roman Virgil, Merlin's knowledge of deeper levels of meaning resulted in him being imbued with the attributes of a magician. Thus he evolved from a half-insane prophet and seer into a wise magician and adviser to Arthur's court.

Although it is possible to separate the various aspects of Merlin's character, the overall portrait remains consistent, suggesting a single figure behind all the strands. Even the various descriptions of his departure from the world bear an overall similarity, despite surface differences.

Merlin and the Fair, Sportive Maid

The reference to "a fair wanton maid" in *Affalannau* may indicate the antiquity of a final theme. This is Merlin's fatal love for the fairy Nimue, sometimes called Niniane or Vivienne, who is generally depicted as having stolen his powers and used them to imprison him, still living, for all time.

We first hear of Nimue, in the guise of Niniane, in the Arthurian compilation known as *The Vulgate Cycle*. This vast collection of story and polemic was written down during the thirteenth century by clerks belonging to the order of Cistercian monks, which was founded by the great medieval theologian Bernard of Clairvaux in 1115. While specifically rendering the material suitable for a Christian readership, *The Vulgate Cycle* also drew upon a vast range of earlier works. It includes a section entitled *Merlin*, which adapted Robert de Boron's version, although it is a far more complex rendition of the story.

Here we read of the forester Dionas, so named because of his devotion to the Roman goddess Diana, and his daughter Niniane, of whom Diana spoke the following prophecy.

> *I grant thee, and so doth the god of the sea and the stars ... that the first female child that thou shalt have shall be much coveted by the wisest man that ever was on earth ... and he shall teach her the most part of his wit and cunning by way of necromancy, in such manner that he shall be so desirous after he hath seen her, that he shall have no power against her wish, and all things that she enquireth he shall teach.*
> *(From the Middle English* Merlin, *modernized by the author)*

Niniane is regarded in some sense as under the aegis of the goddess Diana, just as her father is described as her "god-son," a euphemistic way of saying that he was a worshipper of the goddess. As to the prophecy, it is proved to be accurate in the story that follows, given here in the fifteenth-century account by Sir Thomas Malory:

> *Merlin fell in a dotage on ... one of the damosels of the lake, that hight [was called] Nimue. But Merlin would let her have no rest, but always he would be with her. And ever she made Merlin good cheer till she had learned of him all manner of things that she desired; and he was assotted [besotted] upon her ... and always ... lay about the lady to have her maidenhood, and she was ever passing weary of him, and fain would have been delivered of him because he was a devil's son ... And so on a time it happed that Merlin showed her a rock whereas was a great wonder ... So by her subtle working she made Merlin to go under that stone ... but she wrought ... for him that he came never out for all the craft that he could do. And so she departed and left Merlin.*
>
> *LE MORTE D'ARTHUR*, BOOK IV, CHAPTER ONE

This somewhat unflattering portrayal of the aged Merlin, besotted with the beautiful fairy damsel Nimue—one of the Ladies of the Lake, no less—who cozens him out of his secrets and then uses them to imprison him, seems to echo the general tendency of medieval writers to seek a Christian interpretation to what is, at times, quite primitive pagan material. Thus, as we have seen, Merlin is portrayed as the son of a devil, rather than an otherworldly being, and Nimue, whose father served the goddess Diana, is portrayed as a temptress whose power derives solely from Merlin.

Arthur Rackham's illustration to Sir Thomas Malory's *Le Morte D'Arthur* seen here shows Nimue casting a spell.

Hidden among the tumbled stones at the foot of Hart Fell in Dumfries and Galloway, Scotland, is a cave said to have been Merlin's home after he went mad at the Battle of Arderydd.

Vita Merlini once again takes a somewhat different tack, giving Merlin a sister, Ganeida, whose own wisdom is no less than her brother's. When the moment comes for him to retire from the world, Merlin withdraws, along with Ganeida, to a wonderful observatory with 72 doors and windows, from which they observe the stars and hold lengthy philosophical discussions upon the meaning of creation. Perhaps we may look to this story for the origin of Nimue, transformed from sister to temptress, who thus extracts the Merlin's wisdom by the use of her wiles. The portrayal of Merlin as an old man stems from a misconception—nowhere is his age specifically stated—and he does, in fact, take the forms both of an old man and a youth on more than one occasion. His aging is perhaps indicative that people expect wisdom from the old rather than the young.

Neither is it without significance that the last person to hear the voice of Merlin in Malory's adaptation is Gawain, another

LEFT: Merlin's Grave at Dumbarton, Scotland, is one of several sites where the body of the renowned enchanter is believed to lie.

character who was downgraded within the works of predominantly Christian interpreters. Arthur's nephew, Gawain began life as a thoroughly pagan champion of the Goddess and ended it portrayed as a murderer and a libertine. It seems somehow appropriate that, happening to pass by the great stone under which the mage is imprisoned, it is Gawain who hears "the cry of Merlin" telling him what has occurred and warning that he will not be seen again in Arthur's time.

Merlin's tomb becomes known as the *perron*, or stone, of Merlin, and the Knights of the Round Table often assemble there to begin their adventures. Even in his withdrawn state Merlin influences what occurs in the Arthurian world. The seeds he plants in the early days of Arthur's reign are intended to prepare the way for the great Quest of the Holy Grail—though this was not to begin until several years after his departure from the tales.

In another version of the tales, the medieval *Didot Perceval,* Merlin remarks that he must withdraw because

> *Those who are gathered together here must believe what they see happen and I would not that they should think that I had brought it about.*

This makes it clear that Merlin understood the necessity for Arthur and his followers to stand alone without the benefit of a far-seeing visionary.

The same text gives us the most mysterious version of Merlin's departure. It describes him retreating into an *esplumoir*, a French word that has no precise meaning in English but which can be interpreted to mean to a "moulting cage" where hawks are placed to shed their feathers. Symbolically this is clear enough, Merlin withdraws to shed the form of his current life and to adopt a new, more spiritual garment. From within his moulting cage he is able to see far more then ever before, and his influence extends further, beyond the confines of the Arthurian kingdom into the world at large. He remains, as the psychologist Carl Jung called him, "the age-old son of the mother" able to work toward the integration of mankind with deity—the final aim of all such coworkers with God. For many, Merlin encompasses the greatest wisdom and most profound depths of human endeavor; generations of spiritual seekers have described visions received from the withdrawn Merlin.

Merlin Among the Stars

Merlin's story does not end here. The character has continued to influence writers and storytellers from that day to this. There are elements of his character in such modern icons as Gandalf, from J.R.R. Tolkien's *The Lord of the Rings*, and in Obi Wan-Kenobi and Yoda in George Lucas's epic movie-cycle, *Star Wars*.

Among the modern writers who have developed the figure of Merlin significantly is T.H. White in *The Once and Future King* and *The Book of Merlyn*. His portrayal of the old enchanter as an absent-minded wizard who lives backward has influenced a generation of more recent writers. Mary Stewart's magnificent trilogy of books, *The Crystal Cave*, *The Hollow Hills* and *The Last Enchantment*, give us a modern portrait of Merlin that has seldom been bettered. Her hero is more of a seer than a magician, and the delicate exploration of his relationship to Nimue is full of psychological insight.

The Coming of the King: the First Book of Merlin by Nikolai Tolstoy, sets the story in northern Britain two generations after Arthur's departure, and consists in part of Myrddin's (as he is called here) memoirs, in which he recalls not only the time of Arthur but a mythological era as well. The figure that emerges is, however, probably the closest anyone has got since Geoffrey of Monmouth to the real character of Merlin—immemorially ancient, powerful and almost merging with the land itself:

> *It seemed to King Ceneu and his companions that there arose … a man greater far in stature than the men of their own time. His clothes were but the undressed skins of beasts, his hair thin and grey and flowing, and his aspect paler, emaciated, wild. He lacked his left eye, which was but a puckered, sightless socket. His gaze seemed to portend both pain and anger.*

Actor Sam Neill played Merlin in the 1998 TV mini-series *Merlin*. The production married older stories of Merlin as a prophet with the portrayal of him as a wizard.

LEFT: Merlin's Cave, at Tintagel in Cornwall, has been associated with the enchanter since the Victorian era, when Alfred Tennyson described Merlin finding the infant Arthur by its entrance.

Stephen Lawhead, in his series *The Pendragon Cycle*, follows the outlines of *Vita Merlini* in its general shape and structure, although the character and story of Merlin is developed far beyond the scope of the medieval tale. Here Merlin is both King of Dyfed and a reluctant seer, whose pain and passion in the wilderness is set forth in all its stark reality. The story is told in the first person, and at the very opening of the book Merlin recalls the various ways in which he has been recognized:

> *Emrys is the name I have won among men and it is my own. Emrys, Immortal ... Emrys, Divine ... Emrys Wledig, king and prophet to his people. Ambrosius it is to the Latin speakers, and Embries to the people of Southern Britain and Lloegres ... But Myrddin Emrys am I to the Cymry of the hill-bound fastness of the west.*

His long life, including years of wandering in the wilds of the hills, chronicled, as is his association with Ambrosius, Uther and, finally, Arthur himself. Lawhead's long and intricately woven chronicle places Merlin squarely at the center of the story, linking him both to the dim and distant realm of Atlantis and to the founding of the great Arthurian kingdom, which is so much Merlin's creation. Of all the recent portrayals of Merlin it is perhaps the best and certainly the most moving.

Among the new generation of writers who have added significantly to Arthurian mythology is Charles de Lint, a Canadian whose perceptions of the darkly wooded world of the Celts runs as deep as any previous writer. In his novel *Spiritwalk*, a section appears called "Merlin Dreams in the Mondream Wood." Here one of the characters, Sara Kendell, comes to live in the Tamson House, a kind of gateway between the worlds where figures from the Otherworld enter and depart at will. Here, in the garden of the house, she encounters a mysterious being:

> *In the heart of the garden stood a tree.*
> *In the heart of the tree lived an old man who wore the shape of a red-haired boy with crackernut eyes that seemed as bright as salmon tails glinting up the water ...*
>
> *His was a riddling wisdom, older by far than the ancient oak that housed his body. The green sap was his blood and leaves grew in his hair. In the winter he slept. In the spring, the moon harped a windsong against his antler tines as the oak's boughs stretched its green buds to wake. In the summer, the air was thick with the droning of bees and the scent of wildflowers that grew in stormy profusion where the fat brown bole became root.*
>
> *And in the autumn, when the tree loosed its bounty to the ground below, there were hazelnuts lying in among the acorns.*
>
> THE SECRETS OF A GREEN MAN

This Merlin is old, older perhaps than any of the other Merlins that we have encountered. He is both Arthur's Merlin and Geoffrey's Merlin and something else as well—an Old Earth Man, the Green One, the Walker in the Woods who had been around for as long as the earth itself has existed. De Lint's contribution, though slight in volume, is as significant of the way we regard Merlin today as any other writer in this age or the past.

As we get further from the time when Merlin may have lived, we seem to curve back to a time even earlier, when he was indeed a god, and when the elements that created his character were first stirring in the hearts and minds of the early storytellers. Merlin's journey is in many ways parallel to Arthur's; he brings in a strand of magic and mystery that was less developed in the oldest accounts of both the hero and the mythic king—at least until the height of the Middle Ages. It is to this period, and to the final flowering of the Arthurian mythology, that we turn next.

The face of Merlin looks back at us from this carving on a rock at Alderley Edge in Cheshire, carved by a local stonemason in the 1900s. Merlin is believed to sleep within the hill.

paignons de la table rõde se assirẽt cha
cun en son lieu.

Cellui iour seruirent leans .iiii.
roys ⁊ plusieurs cheualiers. et

THE ROUND TABLE

4

OPPOSITE: Arthur's greatest knights gather at the Round Table in this illumination from a fourteenth-century manuscript.

In olden days of the King Arthur
Of which the Bretons speke great honor,
All was this land full of faerie.

CHAUCER: *THE CANTERBURY TALES*

The Third Arthur: A Medieval Likeness

AT THE BEGINNING OF THE TWELFTH CENTURY, Arthur was still known only in bardic tales and folklore, told by wandering storytellers. These versions were probably rough-and-ready accounts, drawn from historic memories that had become embroidered into the shape of myth. All this was to change however, with the advent of a book that told the story of Arthur in a style recognizably of its time, and effectively created a third Arthur, the romantic hero of countless medieval courtly romances, full of magic, love, warfare, and spirituality.

We have already encountered the author who created this Arthur, and heard how he reshaped the legends of Merlin into a coherent whole. He was now about to do the same for Arthur—his name was Geoffrey of Monmouth. It was he who created a vehicle for the seemingly inexhaustible supply of stories concerning the exploits of Arthur and his heroes by writing *Historia Regum Brittaniae*." Although this work deals with such semi-historical figures such as King Lear, Cassivellaunus and Constantine, it allocates more than half the total space to the lives of Arthur and Merlin.

Geoffrey's book was phenomenally successful in its time, with countless manuscript copies made and distributed throughout England and the rest of Europe. Although his veracity as a historian was attacked, even by his near contemporaries, who referred to him as a "fabulator" (writer of lies), there is more than a kernal of truth in what Geoffrey wrote. As we have seen already, he claimed to have partially "translated" an ancient book in the British tongue, although no trace of this has ever been discovered. Whatever the truth of the matter, there can be no doubt that Geoffrey pulled together strands of oral tradition, historical memory, and pure invention, and dressed them in the fashions and settings of the time. In doing so he created the first Arthurian "novel," and set the seal upon the literary career of his hero for several ages to follow.

Here is part of his description of Arthur's court—from which it can be seen how far Arthur has come from the setting of "Dark-Age" Britain:

LEFT: The Red Knight, a symbol of evil in Terry Gilliam's *The Fisher King* (1991), a fresh take on the story of Arthur and the Quest for the Grail.

> *When the feast of Whitsuntide began to draw near, Arthur … made up his mind to hold a plenary court at that season and place the crown of the kingdom on his head. He decided, too, to summon to this feast the leaders who owed him homage, so that he could celebrate Whitsun with greater reverence and renew the closest possible pacts of peace with his chieftains …*

The feast is held at the City of Legions, Caerleon-on-Usk, and kings and chieftains come from all over Britain, much of Europe, and from Scandinavia, which Arthur has recently conquered. All attend Mass in two great cathedral churches and afterward there is a splendid feast, at which Kay the Seneschal (steward), attended by a thousand noblemen dressed in ermine, bore in the food. Geoffrey continues:

> *If I were to describe everything, I should make this story far too long. Indeed, by this time, Britain had reached such a standard of sophistication that it excelled all other kingdoms in its general affluence, the richness of its decorations, and the courteous behaviour of its inhabitants. Every knight in the country who was in any way famed for his bravery wore livery and arms showing his own distinctive color; and women of fashion often displayed the same colors. They scorned to give their love to any man who had not proved himself three times in battle. In this way the womenfolk became chaste and more virtuous and for their love the knights were ever more daring.*

Here we have the medieval, Christian court of Arthur, with its splendid banquets and its great churches and, of course, its knights and ladies, the former seeking to impress the latter with their prowess in battles. This is not far from the elaborate medieval romances that followed, and which established Arthur as the most important, most widely celebrated king in the Western world.

Geoffrey's work was translated from the original Latin into both Norman French and Anglo-Saxon. A veritable avalanche of Arthurian romances followed, the most famous of which were written toward the end of the twelfth century by a French poet named Chrétien de Troyes. It is to him that we must look for the elements that shaped most of the retellings of Arthurian legend that were to follow.

From Chrétien's prolific pen flowed a series of five tales, written in elegant verse: *Erec and Enid* (*c.* 1170), *Cligés* (*c.* 1176), *Lancelot* (*c.* 1177–81), *Yvain* (*c.* 1171–81) and *The Story of the Grail* (*c.* 1181–90). Within them, much of what we now recognize as the essential core of the Arthurian legends came into being—Chrétien gave us the stories of Arthur's greatest knights, the love affair of Lancelot and Guinevere, and the Quest for the Grail. Though these must have existed earlier in the form of oral tales, it is to Chrétien that we owe the first written versions that have influenced everything Arthurian since.

This illustration from a fifteenth-century French manuscript shows Arthur and his greatest knights.

Chrétien's works are thronged with otherworldly Celtic

RIGHT: In this picture from the fifteenth-century *Book of Sir Lancelot*, the great hero captures the castle of Dolorous Garde using a magic shield from the Lady of the Lake.

characters in new guises and with new names: Edern, son of Nut (Yder), Gilvaethwy, son of Don (Griflet) Gwalchmai (Gawain), Maelwas (Maheloas) and Guigomar. In *Erec and Enid* it is notable that Arthur maintains and revives the ancient magical custom of the hunt for the white stag, in which the hero who kills the wondrous beast, awards its head to his lady and proclaims her the fairest among all the women of the court. This theme, with an attendant episode in which a kiss is bestowed upon the winner, harks back to more primitive origins, in which the hero marries an ancient hag who is then transformed into a fawn, the hero into a buck.

Even *Lancelot*, which on one level tells an elaborate and decorous tale of courtly love, with the hero rescuing his mistress from the hands of a desperate man, is based on the Celtic story that first occurred in the sixth-century *Life of St Gildas*. There, the protagonist was a lord of the Otherworld who carried off Guinevere, not simply out of desire for her, but because she represented the "sovereignty of the land."

Three of the stories retold by Chrétien also appear in the Welsh story cycle, *The Mabinogion*. Debate still rages over whether the French or Welsh versions of the tales are the oldest. It now seems certain that Chrétien wrote his down first, but whoever the anonymous author of the three tales in the Welsh story cycle may have been, he probably drew on the same original source as the French poet, though unlike Chrétien many features of a more primitive nature were retained. These versions, which correspond to *Erec*, *Yvain* and *The Story of the Grail*, therefore actually represent an earlier strand and hark back to the mythical Arthur.

The King of Romance

Arthur's literary career continued unabated for another three hundred years, with countless new stories and retellings appearing throughout Britain and Europe. New characters appeared, or were woven in to the Arthurian ambience. Celtic warriors such as Gwalchmai and Lleminawg, traded their old names and customs for new, and "Gawain" and "Lancelot" became the most widely known and written-about characters in European courtly literature.

One of the translators of Geoffrey of Monmouth's *Historia*, an Anglo-Norman named Wace, added an idea of his own—or one that he had heard—to his version of the book, the *Roman de Brut*, which was completed in 1155:

Arthur held high state in a very splendid fashion. He ordained the courtesies of courts, and bore himself with so rich and noble a bearing, that neither the emperor's court at Rome, nor any other bragged of by man, was accounted as aught besides that of the king. Arthur never heard speak of a knight in praise—but he caused him to be numbered of his household ... Because of these noble lords about his hall, of whom each knight pained himself to be the hardiest champion ... Arthur made the Round Table, so reputed of the Britons. This Round Table was ordained of Arthur that when his fair fellowship sat to meet their chairs should be high alike, their service equal, and none before or after his comrade. Thus no man could boast that he was exalted above his fellow, for all alike were gathered round the board, and none was alien at the breaking of Arthur's bread. At this table sat Britons, Frenchmen, Normans, Angevins, Flemings, Burgundians, and Loherins.

Wace was attempting to bring the most important factions of medieval Europe to Arthur's table—not only the fellowship of British knights, but also the kings and lords of the frequently

A seventeenth-century woodcut of Arthur at the center of the Round Table. With him are Sir Gawain, Sir Tristram, Sir Galahad and Sir Perceval, among others.

warring kingdoms from the European continent. He set a precendent that was to be followed by virtually every medieval writer thereafter.

Within a few years of Wace's book yet another translation of *Historia*, this time into the Anglo-Saxon tongue, appeared from the pen of a writer of whom we know virtually nothing other than his name: Layamon (Lawman). His *Brut* was a rich and sinewy style rendition, and added vivid details of the inception of the Round Table:

Afterward it saith in the tale, that the king went to Cornwall; there came to him anon one that was a crafty workman, and met the king, and fair him greeted: "Hail be thou, Arthur, noblest of kings! I am thine own man; through many land I have gone; I know of treeworks, wondrous many crafts. I heard say beyond the sea new tidings, that thy knights gan to fight at thy board; on a midwinter's day many there fell; for their mickle mood wrought murderous play, and for their high lineage each would be within. But I will thee work a board exceeding fair, that thereat may sit sixteen hundred and more, all turn about, so that none be without; without and within, man against man. And when thou wilt ride, with thee thou mightest it carry, and set it where thou wilt, after thy will; and then thou needest never fear, to the world's end, that ever any moody knight at thy board may make fight, for there shall the high be even with the low." Timber was caused to be brought, and the board to be begun; in four weeks' time the work was completed.

Wace and Layamon were the first writers to mention a Round Table, at which all men sat in equality; but the idea was to remain at the center of Arthurian story from here on. To the Round Table came knights and heroes from all over Europe, forming a glittering fellowship dedicated to the emerging concept of chivalry. The Round Table was a hub around which everything else revolved; adventures began and ended there, distressed women came in search of help in the form of a knight strong enough to overcome all foes. The peace of the king meant that anyone could travel the length and breadth of the land, laden with treasure, without fear of assault. In this we see a development of ideas expressed in the older tales of Arthur, but given a new form. The companies of Celtic warriors, seated in their halls around a central fire, aportioning prime cuts of meat as as mark of honor to each hero, boasting of their deeds and conquests, has evolved into a courtly fellowship where all are equal. The old spur toward valor is channeled into quests and adventures undertaken at the request of those in need.

In addition, the very existence of the Round Table and its growing band of heroes enabled the Arthurian world to open out in every direction, and to become one of the central themes of medieval literature from then onward.

Arthur himself was now widely recognized as a shining example of all that a Christian king should be. When William Caxton published his edition of Malory's *Le Morte D'Arthur* in 1485, he described in his preface how numerous people had reproached him with failing to print a history of "the most renowned Christian King … Arthur, which ought to be remembered among us English men before of all other Christian kings."

Le Morte D'Arthur is possibly the greatest version of the tales to emerge from the medieval era. Malory tells the story of Arthur, from birth to death, in prose that has seldom been equaled. His book was a threnody for the dying age of chivalry, which Arthur and his knights represented above all. It has ensured that the stories of the noble Fellowship of the Round Table have not been forgotten, and that the tradition they embody has remained evergreen.

RIGHT: A tapestry depicting episodes from the story of Tristan and Isolde. Here we see the lovers meeting in the garden behind the back of Isolde's husband, King Mark.

A Table Like the World

Malory's book contains the most coherent account of the saga of Arthur, with all its romantic detail in place. From him we learn how, once the wars that attended Arthur's ascent to the throne were over, he decided to take a wife, and despite Merlin's warnings that she would one day betray him, he selected Guinevere, the daughter of King Leodegrance of Cameliarde. With Guinevere came, as dowry, a great round table, made by Merlin at the bidding of Arthur's father, Uther Pendragon. A table "round in the likeness of the world," at which one hundred and fifty knights could sit, and none seem higher in favor than the rest. And on the day of his marriage Arthur required Merlin to find sufficient knights "which be of most prowess and worship" to fill at least fifty of the seats.

> *This Merlin did, and fifty more came from Leodegrance, so that a hundred sat down together at the table on that first day. And when they had all done homage to Arthur they returned to the Hall where the Round Table stood and found that on the back of each chair was a name, set there in golden letters. The names were all of those already chosen, and many more that were as yet not come. But two remained blank, and of these Merlin would only say that they would be filled in due course.*

Thus the Fellowship of the Round Table met for the very first time on the day of the Arthur's wedding to Guinevere; and if the seeds were already sown for the downfall of Arthur's great dream, if Lancelot's gaze fell too often on the Queen, the shadows were distant on that day. For the fame of the Round Table and its heroes would resound through the ages, inspiring kings of many countries to emulate Arthur, and to found orders of their own in imitation of the Round Table.

The first adventure follows swiftly. As the Fellowship sit at dinner there comes into the hall a white hart, pursued by a white dog and fifty pairs of black hounds. As they race around the table the white dog bites the hart, which leaps high in the air, knocking over a knight sitting nearby. The knight seizes the dog and departs hurriedly. In the next moment a lady rides into the hall and demands that the knight be brought back, for the dog is hers. Before anyone can respond, another fully armed knight rides up, seizes the lady and carries her off by force.

Astonishment, and perhaps some amusement, attends these events. But Merlin stands forth and admonishes the Fellowship not "to leave these adventures so lightly," for they are a challenge from the Otherworld to test the mettle of the newly instated

A contemporary painting of the great castle of Camelot by Anna-Marie Fergusson, from a series of paintings illustrating Sir Thomas Malory's *Le Morte D'Arthur.*

knights, his nephew Sir Gawain, and the illegitimate son of King Pellinore, Sir Tor, out after the white hart and the dog respectively; and Pellinore himself, a tried and trusted warrior, after the lady who has been abducted.

So at the outset this single incident has given rise to three separate adventures, which are then narrated at length. They are to be the first of many such which begin in similiar fashion, with the entry of a knight or a lady into the court, requesting succor or some favor of Arthur and the Fellowship. They cannot refuse, so long as the request is a fair one and the demand honest. For at the end of that first, triple quest, all of the Fellowship swears an oath:

Never to do outrage nor murder, and always to flee treason; also, by no means to be cruel, but to give mercy unto him that asketh mercy, upon pain of forfeiture of their worship and lordship of King Arthur for evermore; and always to do ladies, damosels, and gentlewomen succour, upon pain of death. Also, that no man take no battles in a wrongful quarrell for no law, nor for world's goods. Unto this were all the knights sworn of the Table Round, both old and young. And every year were they sworn at the high feast of Pentecost.

The rules are simple enough and reflect the ideals of medieval chivalry. Being human, not all of the knights keep to these demands placed upon them by their king. But despite some failings, they hold true to the honor of the Round Table, and, as if in answer to their existence, strange events seem to multiply on every side, seeing to it that they never lack the opportunity of being tested and tried.

Later Arthur establishes a custom, whereby at any high feast he will not eat until some wonder or adventure has been related to him. And so begins a pattern, whereby the knights ride "at errantry," wandering hither and thither throughout the land in search of wrongs to right or villainy to combat. Brother knights are rescued, as well as ladies; evil knights are overthrown, and either killed or sent to Arthur to crave pardon. Many of these become Round Table knights themselves, giving up their former pursuits. But there are always others, always further adventures to attempt, as the great knights on their great horses thunder through the forests of Arthur's realm in quest of their king's dream of chivalry and the perfect earthly kingdom.

The Forest of Adventure

Most of the medieval adventures of the Fellowship of the Round Table take place in the setting of deep, primeval forest. This in part reflects the physical appearance of the countryside at the time when most of the romances were written; but there is a deeper significance than this. The forest symbolized an untamed world, where almost anything could, and did, lie in wait for the unwary. It stood, also, for a certain state of mind, a place to be reached on the long road from birth to death—like Dante's impenetrable forest of the mind in which the soul, wakening as he expressed it "midway through life's journey," found itself with a thousand possible ways through the darkness of the world beneath the trees.

The forest, too, was part of the "Otherworld," a vast, uncharted tract that lay along the borders between the world of Middle Earth and the fairy realms. Certain parts were given names: Broceliande, Arden, Inglewood: dark places redolent of enchantment, where only those intent upon adventure would willingly go. Here rode Arthur himself, in pursuit of innocent sport, to be met by the terrifyingly powerful Gromer Somer Jour (Man of the Summer's Day), who could bind him at will and demand that he discover the answer to an impossible question, or face the consequences.

In another story, Guinevere and her escort, Sir Gawain, become separated from the rest of their hunting party and find themselves sheltering near the fearful Tarn Watheling, where more than one adventure begins. There, they witness a horrific apparition, the ghost of Guinevere's mother, who "yammerd" horribly at them, and warned of dread things to come.

Yet though the forest contained many terrors, it contained as many wonders. From its depths came beautiful fairy women, to test and beguile the wandering knights as they plied their course through the trees. Many sought husbands among the knights and sired sons upon them—introducing a strain of otherworldly blood into the company.

One such knight is Sir Launfal, who wanders into the Otherworld, meets and marries a beautiful fairy woman. He swears to keep the marriage secret on pain of losing his love forever. Yet Launfal is unable to keep silent when Queen Guinevere herself approaches him with words of love, and, in desperation, he declares that even she, for all her renowned beauty, is no match for his own dear love.

Earning the enmity of the queen, Launfal faces death or banishment rather than speak further, and is finally vindicated by the appearance of the *fée* herself, who enters the court and outshines every woman there, before carrying Launfal away "to Avalon, it is believed."

Not all such women encountered in the forest were as fair of face and speech. Ragnall, one of many archetypes of the Celtic Goddess, appears as a hideous, "Loathly Lady," who tricks Arthur into promising her Sir Gawain in marriage in return for a favor. Her subsequent appearance at court, her gross manners and appearance, in part prepare one for the transformation that occurs on the wedding night, when Ragnall, who has been "enchanted," is restored to her true beauty through Gawain's love and understanding. These magical women are examined in more detail in the next chapter.

Elsewhere in the depths of the forest roamed the Questing Beast, a creature part lion, part serpent, part goat, which made a sound as though thirty pairs of hounds were in its belly. Arthur first glimpses it as a youth, before he is crowned king, and it —

presages a meeting with Merlin, who appears first as a child, then as an old man, and tells Arthur of his birth and parentage, making many cryptic references to future events. The Questing Beast he does not explain, but we learn that the woman who gave birth to it had condemned a man to be torn to pieces by dogs. It exists solely to be pursued, and is followed for many years by King Pellinore. After his death, a Saracen knight, Palomides, takes up the quest for the beast, but seems never to succeed, for the beast is a *ferlie*, a wonder out of the Otherworld, which cannot be caught or pinned down by any mortal being.

Men and women who had the power to transform themselves into animals are not infrequent in the Arthurian tales. In one story Arthur follows a strange, composite beast that turns into a venerable, white-haired man; another is one of the earliest tales concerning a werewolf, *Bisclavret*. In this story, a knight is betrayed by his wife and her lover, and cursed living as a wolf until, eventually, he returns to human form.

In a Welsh story, *The Lady of the Fountain* we encounter "The Lord of the Beasts," who has one foot, one eye and one arm, and commands all the beasts of the forest, who gather about him like a congregation listening to a sermon. When the knight Kynon asks him what power he has over the animals, he replies:

> *"I will show thee, little man," said he. And he took his club in his hand, and with it he struck a stag a great blow so that he brayed vehemently, and at his braying the animals came together, as numerous as the stars in the sky … and he looked at them, and bade them go and feed; and they bowed their heads, and did him homage as vassals to their lord.*

Such ancient, mythic characters are the legacy of the older Arthurian world; the realms of fairy and those of Arthur overlap at every point. Even in the Quest for the Grail, which is examined in Chapter Six, and which is perhaps the greatest challenge to the Fellowship of the Round Table, the themes of the pagan Otherworld are threaded like a strand of green through the scarlet tapestry of Christian miracle and dream.

The Greatest Fellowship in the World

From the Lands Adventurous to the Black Pine, to the Fountain of Barenton, hidden deep in the Valley of No Return, the Knights of the Round Table rode "overthwart and endlong" the length and breadth of the land. Wherever the marvellous menagerie of the knight's heraldic devices—eagles, bulls, ravens and lions—appeared, they were recognized, and their aid or company sought. Like the legendary "fast guns" of the American West, they were sought out by those wishing to prove themselves the most chivalrous in the land—maybe even earn for themselves a seat at the Round Table.

Two great families provided many of the leading figures of the Arthurian cycle: those of Orkney and those of de Galles. The Orkney clan—Gawain, Gaheries, Agravain and Gareth—were the sons of King Lot of Orkney and his Queen Morgause, who was Arthur's half-sister and the mother of the bastard Mordred. The de Galles family—Perceval, Lamorack and Aglovale—were the sons of King Pellinore (the mother is not named) who had also numerous illegitimate by-blows—including the Sir Tor who took part in the first adventure of the Round Table. Pellinore also had a legitimate daughter who is sometimes named Dindraine, and who plays an important part in the Quest for the Grail. Between them they account for more than half the main storylines in the Arthurian saga.

But there was much rivalry between these two families, sparked by the killing of Lot of Orkney by Pellinore, after which the Orkney faction, led by Gawain, carried out several murderous vengeance attacks on the household of de Galles. The death of Queen Morgause followed at the hands of her own son, Gaheries, after she became the lover of Lamorack, whom the brothers slew soon after. The war between the two households continues throughout the reign of Arthur, providing a dark thread against the glorious deeds of the remainder of the Fellowship.

Despite such internecine struggles, the Round Table remained a mirror of all that was best in humanity and was recognized as far more than a meeting place for the knights. So universally was it admired that several orders of chivalry, with kings casting themselves in the role of Arthur, were created. To this day we may see one of the products of this idea in the shape of the "Round Table," currently in the Great Hall at Winchester, on which the figure of Henry VIII appears in the guise of Arthur.

In an attempt to claim the Round Table for a higher authority, the Burgundian poet Robert de Boron, tracking backward again as he had done in the story of Merlin, added a further dimension—that of the spiritual. The Table of Arthur, he declared, was made in the likeness of two earlier tables. The first, at which Christ and the Apostles sat to celebrate the Last Supper, had been copied by the Grail kings as a suitable resting place for the Holy Cup itself, of which they were guardians and keepers. Merlin built the third table, at which the Fellowship would meet until the Holy Grail itself appeared and sent them forth on the greatest quest of all, for which they had long been prepared.

But despite repeated attempts to render the tales in a Christian fashion, many of the most powerful adventures of the Fellowship begin with the appearance at Arthur's court of one of the magical, otherworldly women who hold the keys to so much of the action. We have encountered them before in our journey; it is time to meet them properly and to find out something of the role they play in the great pattern of myth and romance that is the Arthurian tradition.

RIGHT: In this fifteenth-century painting from *The Book of Lancelot*, King Arthur and his knights assemble to witness the first appearance of the Grail at Camelot.

House of de Galles

The House of the Pendragon

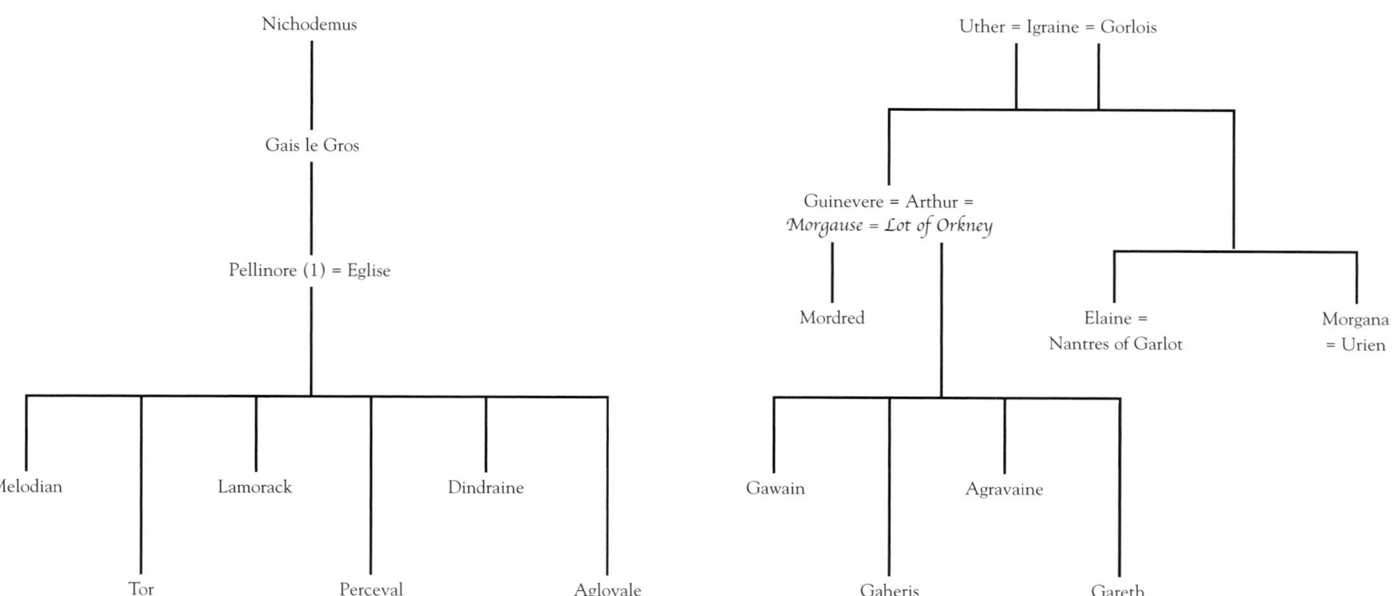

LADIES OF THE LAKE

OPPOSITE: This portrait of *The Damsel of the Lake, called Nimue the Enchantress*, painted by Frank Cadogan Cowper (1877–1958) shows her in vain mode, admiring her image in a mirror.

And near him stood the Lady of the Lake,
Who knows a subtler magic than his own –
Clothed in white samite, mystic, wonderful,
She gave the king his huge crosshilted sword …

ALFRED TENNYSON: *THE COMING OF ARTHUR*

Goddesses in Disguise

THE WOMEN OF THE ARTHURIAN LEGENDS are every bit as important as their male counterparts—some might say even more important as they frequently initiate new adventures. They are also, in many cases, the holders of the magical power and secrets of the realm. Thus it is the Lady of the Lake who brings Arthur his magical sword, Excalibur, and who continues to aid him throughout his kingship, while Morgan le Fay becomes his bitterest foe and does everything in her power to destroy him.

The reason why these otherworldly women are considered so important within the Arthurian cycle is that they were once regarded as goddesses. That this is not immediately apparent is due to the gradual Christianization of the material, and to the changing attitudes of successive generations of storytellers who altered and sometimes suppressed the pagan aspects of the tales they told.

But there was a great deal that survived—a testimony to the strength of the original traditions on which so much of the

OPPOSITE: While Merlin looks on, the Lady of the Lake offers to give Arthur the magical sword Excalibur, in this painting by William Hetherall.

BELOW: The Lady of the Lake greets Merlin and Arthur in this nineteenth-century woodcut.

Arthurian saga was founded. The reality behind the Ladies of the Lake and the otherworldly women who throng the pages of Arthurian tales, leads back again and again to the sometimes fearsome goddesses of Celtic tradition.

The Lady of the Lake herself, who plays an important role in the story of Arthur, remains nameless in all but one text: Layamon's *Brut*. Layamon, who was writing in the twelfth century, seems to have had access to older traditions that do not appear elsewhere. When he describes the birth of Arthur for example, he adds some significant details:

There Uther the king took Ygaerne for queen; Ygaerne was with child by Uther the king, all through Merlin's craft, before she was wedded. The time came that was chosen, then was Arthur born. So soon as he came on earth, elves took him; they enchanted the child with magic most strong, they gave him might to be the best of all knights; they gave him another thing, that he should be a rich king; they gave him the third, that he should live long; they gave to him the princely virtues most good, so that he was most generous of all men alive. This the elves gave him, and thus the child thrived.

One of the many women who fell in love with Sir Lancelot was the innocent Elaine of Astolat, seen here hurrying toward the hut where the knight lies sick.

When Lancelot refused her, Elaine of Astolat ("The Lady of Shallot") gave up her life and commanded that her body be laid in a barge, which floated downriver to Camelot.

Later, when Arthur lies mortally wounded, he declares that he will

> *fare to Avalun, to the fairest of all maidens, to Argante the queen, an elf most fair, and she shall make my wounds all sound; make me all whole with healing draughts.*

This reference makes it fairly clear that the Lady of the Lake is an elf, and that she may have been a foster mother to Arthur. Nowhere else does the name Argante appear in connection with her, and Layamon may have been thinking of the French *argent* (silver) to describe her, though it is more likely that the name derives from a more distant Celtic original. Most other versions of this episode replaced Argante with Morgan, a curious fact when one considers she is Arthur's lifelong adversary.

The Child of the Lake

One of the primary roles of the Lady of the Lake is that of a foster mother. Chrétien de Troyes describes her as the protector and foster mother of another great hero—Lancelot—in his poem *The Knight of the Cart.* When Lancelot is caught between the postern-gate and the portcullis while trying to escape from a castle, he raises to his eyes a ring that the Lady of the Lake had given him and prays to her exactly as a knight of the time might petition the Virgin Mary—or indeed a goddess.

> *"Lady, lady, so help me God, I'm now in great need of you to come to my help." That lady was a fairy who had given him the ring and brought him up as a child; and he had every confidence that, wherever he might be, she would help and rescue him.*

One major text that speaks extensively of the Lady of the Lake as foster mother is a twelfth-century romance called *Lanzelet*, which was written by a Swiss knight, Ulrich von Zatzikhoven. It clearly draws upon much earlier traditions about the Otherworld.

Zatzikhoven's story tells how King Pant of Genewis is besieged by enemies and driven from his home, wounded, with his wife Clarine and their year-old son. Clarine watches her husband die and then hides in a tree. Then, "there came a fay of the sea, with a mist like a wind, and took the child from the queen and carried it with her into her land." The sea-fay, described as a *merfeine* (mermaid), appears in the nick of time, for the enemies return to capture Clarine.

The mermaid proves to be the Queen of Maidenland (who is also the Lady of the Lake), where the prevailing season is Maytime. The mountain stronghold on which the queen's castle stands is made of crystal, and is situated on an impregnable island that can only be reached by a diamond bridge. There the child Lanzalet is taught the courtly arts of music and singing. The queen also sends for mermen to teach the boy sword-play, wrestling, hurling, jumping, archery, hawking and hunting. He grows to be 15 years old but has never ridden a horse. In order to acquire this skill he asks to leave Maidenland.

He begs the Queen to tell him his name and lineage, which have been hidden from him, but she refuses until he has promised to overcome Iweret of Beforet (the beautiful forest). If he accomplishes this, she will give him his name. To this end, she gifts him with white armor, a sword and a shield with a golden eagle painted on it.

After many encounters and adventures, the youth finds the Castle of Death where Mabuz the Cowardly lives. Mabuz turns out to be the son of the Queen of Maidenland. It was prophesied to her before his birth that he should always be cowardly. The queen accordingly built Mabuz a castle now called *Schatel le Mort*, (Castle of Death), which magically sustains his courage, but saps the strength and hope of all else who enter it. Lanzelet goes in to the castle and is thrown into the dungeon. Iweret has taken Mabuz's lands, and reports of further incursions are brought. Mabuz promises to keep his hostages unharmed for a year if Lanzelet will ride out against Iweret and overcome him.

Lanzelet overcomes Iweret and marries his only daughter, Yblis. No sooner has he fulfilled the Queen's command, than one of her ladies appears and gives Lanzelet his name and lineage. He gives the lady of Maidenland a ring, which has a magical property—no one can refuse anything of its wearer.

Lanzelet proves to be Arthur's nephew and takes Yblis to court. Thence comes the Queen of Maidenland's messenger carrying a magic mantle with the instruction that whomever it fits shall be its possessor. The mantle is tried on by various ladies, including Guinevere, but it magically shortens on most of them, due, says the mermaid-messenger, to some fault in that lady's affections. Yblis at length tries it on and it fits her perfectly. So it is that the Queen of Maidenland acclaims the worthiness of her fosterling's wife.

Lanzelet wins back his lands and honors his mother, after which he is brought the arms of Iweret by a messenger—a wondrous sword and a magical providing net: a suitable gift for a knight raised in the watery queendom of Maidenland. He and Yblis have four children.

In this story Lanzelet at first has no name and no arms, until given them by the Queen of Maidenland, though he does gain a wife. The inhuman character of the fairy-abduction is stressed throughout *Lanzelet*, where the hero is taken into custody in order to compensate for the Queen of Maidenland's own son, Mabuz, who is, to all intents and purposes, a changeling. The changeling theme tells of an ugly fairy-child left in a mortal cradle in exchange for a beautiful mortal baby. The Queen of Maidenland has no compunction in stealing Lanzelet for her own ends.

The theme of losing a child and acquiring another one is typical of fairy abductions. The fairy-kind deposit their own ill-favored children with mortals and abduct good-looking children into fairies. Another common Celtic theme is the hero's adoption by an otherworldly woman who teaches him arms: the Irish hero Fionn Mac Cumail is brought up by the druidess Bodhmall and the huntress Liath Luachra; while the warrior Cuchulainn is trained by Scathach, the eponymous goddess of the Isle of Skye. The Queen of Maidenland is responsible for giving Lanzelet the best possible education in arms, though she neglects riding—that mainstay of chivalry—because she does not wish her fosterling to leave Maidenland until he is old enough to accomplish her ends.

The Lady of the Lake is thus revealed as a prime mover behind the scenes in many of the major events that take place within the Arthurian world. Shadowy and always mysterious, she remains, like Merlin, a motivating force behind much of the action in the stories — giving magical gifts and advice, testing the knights and even the king himself, while seldom appearing in person. Without her, many of the stories would take completely different direction, and the Arthurian world would certainly be a poorer place.

The Dark Goddess

If the Lady of the Lake is one of Arthur's greatest helpers, his half-sister Morgan le Fay is the exact opposite. Throughout most of the Arthurian saga she is his bitterest foe, constantly sending emissaries to challenge him and several times attempting to have him killed. Morgan is often seen to hate Arthur because his father, Uther, killed her father, Gorlois, in order to marry her mother, Ygaerne. However, the reality lies somewhat deeper than this.

Morgan can be traced back to no less than three Irish goddesses: the Morrigan, Macha and Badbh, all of them battle goddesses, and although, in the medieval Arthurian world, she is described as a mere enchantress, she never loses this connection with war and death. Malory says that after her father's death, and the events of Arthur's birth engineered by Merlin, she was "put to school in a nunnery, where she became a great clerk of necromancy."

It is easy to see, in this statement, a reference to earlier times, when female children who displayed a talent for the second sight, or other aptitudes for the mystical life, were sent to be educated in the schools of priestesses that once flourished in both Britain and Ireland. Morgan, who became known by the epithet "le Fay" (the Fairy), retained many of her goddessly qualities, even in the medieval tales.

This is borne out even in the comparatively late version of her story found in *Le Morte D'Arthur*. On the one hand Morgan is portrayed as an enchantress and shapeshifter, who consistently opposes Arthur's attempts to fashion an exemplary kingdom. On the other hand, she figures as one of the three mysterious queens who appear after the battle of Camlan to bear the wounded Arthur to Avalon, "there to be healed of his wounds." This seeming contradiction, which causes us to wonder which side Morgan is really on, dates back to her true origins when, as a goddess rather than a mortal woman, she would have been far more impartial.

LEFT: Morgan is shown in her magical barge in this painting by Stuart Littlejohn.

The Nine Sisters

Geoffrey of Monmouth, once again recording an ancient tradition, tells us more about Morgan when he refers, in *Vita Merlini*, to nine sisters who dwell on an island in the sea called "The Fortunate Isle," or the Island of Apples, for which we may read Avalon. He continues:

> *She who is first of them is more skilled in the healing art, and excels her sisters in the beauty of her person. Morgan is her name, and she has learned what useful properties all the herbs contain, so that she can cure sick bodies. She also knows an art by which to change her shape, and to cleave the air on new wings like Daedalus.*

This is echoed in Malory's account, where Morgan makes use of her shape-shifting ability by turning herself and her followers into rocks when they are pursued by Arthur and his knights. Her skill as a healer was always legendary.

Geoffrey's description of the wondrous island, with its sisterhood of nine, is accurate in many details to other accounts of the Celtic Otherworld. It is clear enough that he recognizes Morgan as the tutelary spirit, or goddess, of this place, and that her animosity toward Arthur (who, as her half-brother, also has fairy blood) is here an aspect of the challenging and testing role that such figures eternally offer in order to discover who among their many followers is truly worthy of favor.

Morgan appears again in this guise in the marvellous fourteenth-century poem *Sir Gawain and the Green Knight,* where she is the organizing principle behind the appearance of the monstrous green giant at Camelot. The story is typical of the role fulfilled by such goddesses in Arthurian literature, and is worth retelling for the light it throws upon them.

The Green Knight

Arthur's court is assembled for the Christmas feast, but before it can begin there is a crash of thunder and in through the door rides a monstrous figure wielding a mighty axe. He is green from head to foot—green skin, green clothes, green horse. Mocking the assembly he offers to play "a Christmas game" with anyone who has the courage. The rules are as follows: that he will receive a blow with his own axe from any man there, on the understanding that he will gave one back afterward. At first no one comes forward, but when Arthur himself rises from his place, his young nephew Gawain steps forward to accept the challenge. He strikes a single blow, severing the Green Knight's head from his body. But to everyone's horror the giant picks up his head, holds it on high, and the lips move. He will expect Gawain in a year at the Green Chapel. Setting the head once more on his shoulders he departs as he came.

This contemporary painting by Meg Falconer shows the Green Knight's great axe, used in the "Beheading Game."

This modern illustration by Paul Bonner shows Gawain taking a blow from his fearsome opponent.

A year passes and Gawain prepares to set forth to keep his word. He has no idea of the whereabouts of the Green Chapel, and his wanderings take him into the Wilderness of Wirral, where he faces danger from trolls and the harsh winter weather. Half dead from cold and fatigue he arrives at last at the castle of Sir Bercilak, a huge, larger-than-life figure who offers him hospitality and introduces him to his beautiful wife, who is accompanied by a hideous old woman. Bercilak declares that he knows where the Green Chapel is, a mere few hours' ride away, and declares his intention of going hunting. When Gawain declines to accompany his host, preferring to rest, Bercilak proposes a sporting exchange of winnings: he will give Gawain whatever spoil he derives from the day's hunting, in exchange for anything his guest has won during the same period.

Once Bercilak has departed, his wife enters Gawain's room and attempts to seduce him. Gawain politely refuses, but is forced to accept a single kiss. When Bercilak returns with the spoils of the hunt, all that Gawain has to exchange is the kiss. The same thing happens on the two successive days, the lady of the castle amorously approaches her guest, who accepts first two then three kisses, which he duly exchanges with his host. On the third day, he confesses that he has little chance of surviving his meeting with the Green Knight, at which Lady Bercilak offers him a green baldric (sash) which protects its wearer from all harm. This Gawain accepts, with some hesitation, but does not declare it in his day's "winnings."

Next morning Gawain sets out for the Green Chapel, and on arrival finds the Green Knight sharpening his axe. Gawain kneels in the snow and his adversary twice feints, until Gawain is angered and bids him strike once and for all. The third blow merely nicks Gawain's neck, at which he leaps up declaring honor satisfied and calling on the Green Knight to defend himself. The giant laughs and says that the "game" is over, and that he is really Sir Bercilak, enchanted into his present shape by the arts of "Morgane the goddess," who is really the old crone at the castle. Her intention had been to frighten Guinevere, and to test the strength of Arthur's knights. Gawain has come through with his honor unstained, except for accepting the green baldric from Lady Bercilak, for which reason he received the blow from the Green Knight's axe. Gawain returns to Camelot and tells his story. Arthur's knights all decide to wear green sashes in honor of Gawain's successful adventure.

In this extraordinary tale, which derives from an ancient Irish story, Morgan's role is made to seem slight by the poet, who sought a Christian allegory in what was, essentially, a pagan midwinter tale. Yet even he called Morgan "the goddess," as did at least two other medieval writers. It is clearly Morgan's presence that motivates the story, which concerns nothing less than an initiation designed specifically to test Gawain, and through him the Fellowship of the Round Table. The hero is prepared for an even greater glory, when he becomes the "Knight of the Goddess," her champion and lover in the realms of men.

The Knight of the Goddess

So many of the magical beings who appear at Arthur's court are otherworldly women, usually in disguise. They begin as supplicants but end as initiators. They also fulfill the important role of teacher, preparing the knights for their entry into the world. Among the main protagonists of the Fellowship of the Round Table both Lancelot and Perceval are specifically described as being brought up by women. Lancelot's son, Galahad, who will one day achieve the Quest for the Grail, is put into the charge of nuns when he is born. Gawain, who is both Arthur's nephew and his heir, fulfils an even older role, that of Knight of the Goddess.

We can see traces of this in the Green Knight poem. The theme is elaborated even more in another fourteenth-century poem *The Wedding of Sir Gawain and Dame Ragnall,* which introduces us to another of the primary otherworldly women of the Arthurian world. In this poem Gawain is required to marry the hideously ugly Ragnall in order to save Arthur from death at the hands of the fearsome Gromer Somer Jour. The rest of the story reveals far more of the complex relationship between men and women in the Arthurian world.

When, on their wedding night, Gawain suddenly finds that his hideous bride has become a ravishingly beautiful woman, he is given a further choice: to have her fair by night and foul by day, or vice versa. His response is to allow her to choose, and the spell is thus broken because Gawain gave her "sovereignty"—the right to be herself and to express her own nature—a rare enough thing in the repressive Middle Ages.

Behind this curious tale we catch a glimpse of the age-old theme in which the Goddess of Sovereignty herself encounters the new, young king and by testing him, proves his worthiness to rule. In the version outlined above Gawain acts as Arthur's surrogate, and is, at the same time, established as the Champion of the Goddess, who through him offers her blessing upon the land.

Her choice of Gawain, Arthur's nephew, is not out of place, since to the Celts the relationship of sister's son was considered of equal or even greater worth than patrimony. We may see in this a natural concomitant of the act where Arthur begets a child upon his half-sister Morgause. In the romances she is Morgan's sister, but it is easy to detect the presence of a single figure behind both—the Goddess of the Land, testing the young king, preparing his successor. In this instance Mordred, the offspring of this union, becomes Arthur's nemesis—on one level because to the medieval writers who described this episode incest was a terrible sin, but on another because, in his pride, Arthur refused to acknowledge the right, by Celtic law, of his sister's son to rule after him.

The Flower Bride

In *Gawain and the Green Knight* we learn that the reason why Morgan sent the Green Knight to Arthur's court was to frighten Guinevere. One of the reasons for this was an old rivalry, dating from the beginning of Arthur's reign when Guinevere had

Guinevere was of otherworldly blood, according to the oldest versions of the Arthurian saga. In this painting by Eleanor Fortescue Brickdale, she is walking near Camelot.

banished one of Morgan's lovers from court, thus beginning long-term hostilities. However, there is another rivalry between the two—that of two goddesses of very different aspect.

Morgan, as her origin in the savage figure of the Morrighan indicates, is a dark goddess, representing the powerful earthy qualities of winter and warfare. Guinevere, on the other hand, who was also once recognized as a goddess among the Celts, is known as the "Flower Bride," who represents spring, the unfolding of life and the burgeoning of growth. As such, these two are polarized opposites, and it is even possible to see, in the story of Guinevere's love for Lancelot, who becomes her champion, a pattern of the elemental struggle between the champions of summer and winter for the hand of the Spring Maiden.

A version of this story is told in one of the pre-Arthurian tales found in *The Mabinogion*. It tells of Pwyll, who changes places for a year with Arawn, the Lord of the Otherworld, and undertakes, as one of Arawn's ritual tasks, an annual fight with Hafgan (Summer Song) for the possession of Creiddylad, the Maiden of Spring. We may judge the importance of this theme from the fact that echoes were still to be found as late as the nineteenth century in Wales, where teams of people led by a Lord of Summer and a Lord of Winter, engaged in mock battle for the Maiden.

This last event is significant for a number of reasons. In the story of the Flower Bride she is often stolen away by one of her suitors, to be rescued by the other—thus forming an endless shifting pattern that reflects a continuing seasonal change. In the case of Guinevere we have a clear indication of her having at one time fulfilled this role when we look at the story of her abduction from the *Life of Gildas*.

In this version of the story Guinevere is carried off by a character named Melwas, whom the text calls the King of the Summer Country—a name for the Otherworld. In the later, medieval accounts he is known as Meleagraunce, the son of King Bagdemagus of Goirre or Gor, both names for the Otherworld. Hence we have a scenario in which Guinevere is carried off into the Otherworld by its king or his representative, to be rescued by her champion. The Flower Bride is brought back in triumph to the court of her lord, who is King of the Land. Thus an ancient ritual enactment continues in the Arthurian stories as a story of human desire and jealousy.

RIGHT: *Lancelot and Guinevere,* by Yvonne Gilbert, shows the Queen wearing a wreath of blossoms, identifying her with the ancient Celtic archetype of the Flower Bride.

The Fair Unknown

Once one begins to look one cannot help but see the multiplicity of incidents where women—usually otherworldly women—are either the cause of an adventure, test or trial undertaken by the knights, or act as helpers and guides along the way. One story in particular demonstrates this perfectly.

Sir Thomas Malory, in *Le Morte D'Arthur*, tells the "Tale of Sir Gareth," in which the hero is Gawain's youngest brother, the son of Morgause and Lot of Orkney. Despite his noble birth he chooses to remain incognito on his arrival at Arthur's court, and begs, as the first of three gifts from the King, to be fed for a year. The testy Sir Kay, who takes charge of him, puts him in the kitchens and generally mocks him, naming him "Beaumains" (Fair Hands) because of his unusually large white hands. Both Lancelot and Gawain befriend him in the first year, though the latter does not even recognize his brother.

At the end of the year a damsel named Lynette appears asking for a champion for her sister against Sir Ironside, the Red Knight of the Red Launds, who is besieging her castle. Gareth, alias Beaumains, now makes his two further requests: that he is given this adventure and that Lancelot should follow him and make him a knight when he deems the youth has earned it. Arthur agrees and Gareth and Lynette set out together, the maiden riding ahead and scorning anything to do with the "kitchen knave" that King Arthur has seen fit to send with her.

During the succeeding days Gareth proves himself a sterling fighter, finally even bringing Lancelot, who has followed, to a halt—at which point the great French knight declares Gareth a worthy opponent and knights him on the spot. Despite this, Lynette continues to upbraid her young escort, giving him the benefit of a tongue-lashing at every opportunity. Gareth however, staunchly refuses to be drawn and performs ever more extraordinary deeds of prowess as he encounters a succession of knights in variously colored armor—finally defeating the Red Knight of the Red Launds himself and winning for himself the undying love of Lynette's sister Lyonors.

The story does not end there however. Lyonors bids her champion go forth to win even more honor before he marries her; then, when he has gone, changes her mind and requests her brother to lure him back again by pretending to kidnap a dwarf who has served him faithfully. Eventually all are reconciled and Gareth would have consummated his love before the wedding had not Lynette prevented it by magical means. Lyonors holds a great tournament in which Gareth wears a magic ring enabling him to change the color of his armor at will. He thus fights several Round Table knights in disguise, then slips away unnoticed. Gawain sets out to discover the identity of the young knight who carried all before him and the two brothers meet and fight before Lynette arrives and stops them by identifying them to each other. She then heals their wounds with her magic and they return to the court, where Gareth is recognized as the son of Morgause and Lot and marries Lyonors at a splendid feast.

This story is one of several which tell of "The Fair Unknown," generally the son of a great hero who appears at court incognito, has various adventures, fights with his own brother or father, and is finally recognized and honored by all. In each of these there is also a figure not unlike Lynette, who leads the hero through a series of adventures designed to test his skill and prowess. Almost without exception she possesses magical abilities and is active in arranging his eventual recognition.

Lynette herself actually appears under the name Lunete in another major story from the cycle *Yvain*, by Chrétien de Troyes. Here she rescues the hero several times from death and gives him a ring that conveys the power of invisibility. A passage from Chrétien's poem makes her true identity clear:

> *I would like to make a brief mention of the friendship that was struck up in private between the Moon and the Sun. Do you know of whom I want to tell you? The man who was chief of the knights and honored above them all should indeed be called the Sun. I refer to my lord Gawain … And by the Moon I mean she who is so uniquely endowed with good sense and courtly ways … her name is Lunete."*

Once again we may recognize the figure of the goddess or otherworldly woman who, once we have identified her, seems to appear in a hundred different guises throughout Arthurian tradition. These characters stand behind so much of the action and adventure in the stories—whether as Morgan, sending a magical cloak that consumes to ashes anyone who puts it on, or as Ragnall, setting Gawain the supreme test of courtesy and love, or as any one of a hundred tests and trials undertaken by the knights. She also offers another, supreme test—that of fidelity in love and of devotion to the beloved.

The Cult of Love

The treatment of love in the Arthurian cycles ranges from the openly sensual to the deeply mystical. The character of Gawain, who began life as an heroic figure dedicated to the service of the feminine principle and ended it as a libertine, exemplifies the

way in which shifting cultural forces changed the way successive generations of writers chose to depict love.

By the time the full glory of Arthurian literature reached its peak in the Middle Ages, love had begun to be seen as virtually a cult, sometimes known as "courtly love," which possessed all the trappings of religion and treated all women as goddesses. In the stories and romances written at this time, the initiators into this cult were the otherworldly women of the Arthurian cycle. Heroes such as Lancelot and Tristan—another knight who suffered on account of an illicit passion for a queen of Cornwall—came to exemplify aspects of courtly love. Lancelot is essentially a man of honor, whose very real pain at the betrayal of the king he loves and serves makes him the most human of the characters in the cycle. From the very beginning, once he has recognized the love

Aubrey Beardsley's illustration to Sir Thomas Malory's *Le Morte D'Arthur* shows Morgan le Fay giving Sir Tristram a magical shield to protect him in a forthcoming tournament.

that he shares with Guinevere, he loses no opportunity to be away from the court—becoming, with each successive adventure, both more honored and more desirable to women. Yet despite himself he is helpless, returning again and again to Guinevere like a falcon to the lure. Tristan is a far more amoral figure altogether, successfully cuckolding King Mark of Cornwall for years, and continually resorting to trickery in order to be with his mistress, Isolde.

Malory, in his unique fashion, sums it all up perfectly:

> *... like as winter rasure doth alway arase and deface green summer, so fareth it by unstable love in man and woman. For in many persons there is no stability; for we may see all day, for a little blast of winter's rasure, anon we shall deface and lay apart true love for little or naught, that cost much thing ... But the old love was not so; men and women could love together seven years ... and then was love, truth and faithfulness: and lo, in like wise was used love in King Arthur's days.*

The faithfulness of a lover to his beloved seems more important here than that of husband to wife, and, indeed, so it was held by a majority of people in a time when marriages were arranged for political or financial reasons rather than for love. The teachings of the troubadours, who wandered through most of Europe during the time when the popularity of the Arthurian cycle was at its height, are to be felt in almost every part of the stories of Lancelot and Tristan. For them, love was impossible between married people, and they placed the figure of the beloved on a pedestal, from which it was not to be dislodged until the reactionary backlash of the seventeenth-century puritan ethic.

RIGHT: Roche Rock in Cornwall is, according to local tradition, the place from which Tristan made a dramatic escape from King Mark's men.

BELOW: Tristan and Isolde drink a magical love potion that will ensure they are forever bound to each other, in this fourteenth-century illumination from *The Book of Tristan*.

A Certain Inborn Suffering

In the twelfth century, when courtly love was at its height, a clerk in the service of Marie de Champagne, daughter of the great Queen Eleanor of Aquitaine, composed a book of rules that codified the conventions governing the lover's every act. He called it *The Art of Courtly Love*, and in it he gives a very different definition to that of Malory nearly three hundred years later:

> *Love is a certain inborn suffering derived from the sight of and excessive meditation on the beauty of the opposite sex, which causes each one to wish above all things the embraces of the other and by common desire to carry out all of love's precepts in the other's embrace.*

This certainly describes the intensity of passion evinced by both the great heroes and their royal loves, though it fails to plumb the mystery that fueled both.

In the end, then, human passion becomes inspiration, and we may see behind this a deeper message, which leads back to influence of the otherworldly women, ever seeking to transform Arthur's knights from adventurers into something finer. A passage from the *Perceval* of Chrétien de Troyes, in which Gawain refers to Guinevere, makes much within the stories of Lancelot and Tristan grow clear:

> *Just as the wise master teaches young children, my lady the queen teaches and instructs every living being. From her flows all the good in the world, she is its source and origin. Nobody can take leave of her and go away disheartened, for she knows what each person wants and the way to please each according to his desires.*

This is to say clearly what all the troubadours and their ilk were saying in every song and poem they wrote, that it is the divine element within all women that serves to fuel and inspire men to heights beyond their normal reach. Thus chivalry itself is informed by love, just as love is informed by the service required by all who take the vows of chivalry seriously. Love itself thus becomes an initiation, which is why we find so many of the women who feature largely within the Arthurian cycles to be of otherworldly stock.

The Dream of the Otherworld

It is impossible to explore these ideas without reference to the Otherworld—the home of the Ladies of the Lake. In the stories the knights are constantly wandering out of the world of men and into this place of magic and wonder, the deep-seated urge to go there seeming to derive from a longing for the "other." It was a desire for a place where the laws of the natural world no longer mattered, where anything was possible, and even the poor might become rich, or the dispossessed get back their lost standing in the eyes of the world. This dream was to be replaced by another—a longing for heaven, the place where the good were assured of an eternity of rest and peace. The Celtic Otherworld was altogether a more robust place, where the simplest pleasures—ample food and drink, beautiful women, great combats in which neither opponent received fatal wounds—abounded. One place above all summed up this otherworldliness more than any other. It was the place to which Arthur was fated to go to be healed of his wounds by the nine sisters. Its name is Avalon, and it is the first and oldest home of the Ladies of the Lake.

The Isle of Apples

Among all the hundreds of names attached to the Celtic Otherworld, that of Avalon must be the most evocative. Many have sought to discover the whereabouts of this fabled place, and, since the Middle Ages, tradition has associated it with the Somerset town of Glastonbury, which has been called "this holiest earth." Here, despite its earlier, pagan associations, Joseph of Arimathea is believed to have come, bearing the Holy Grail, and established the first Christian community in Britain within living memory of Christ.

It may be unwise to seek a physical place for something as elemental as Avalon. However, before Glastonbury (a Saxon name), in the time of the Celtic warlords when Somerset was known as "The Summer Country" and was portrayed as more than half in the Otherworld, the site was known by another name: *Yniswitrin*, The Island of Glass. In that time, before the coming of Arthur, it was ruled over by Avalach, who is also called *Rex Avalonis*—the King of Avalon. Here he is the father of Morgan, who is herself described as "The Royal Virgin of Avalon"—a title that has a hereditary ring to it.

Avalon was a place where eternity touched the earth, where anything could happen—and did. It was both a gateway between the worlds, and the home of the deepest mysteries of Britain. It was one of "The Fortunate Isles," a place of apple trees drenched in the perfume of flowers. It was a place of healing, a realm of peace where even the enmity of Morgan for Arthur no longer held good. Here, too, belongs Nimue, the damsel of the Lake who in some stories enchanted Merlin and finally imprisoned

LEFT: The fairy Nimue watches as Merlin descends the stairs into an underground chamber in which she will shortly imprison him.

him in a cavern beneath a great rock.

Another early text, *Gesta Regnum Britanniae*, describes Avalon in terms that link it even more explicitly to the fairy realms:

This wondrous island is girdled by the ocean; it lacks no good things; no thief, reiver or enemy lurks in ambush there. No snow falls; neither summer nor winter rages uncontrollably, but unbroken peace and harmony and the gentle warmth of unbroken spring. Not a flower is lacking, neither lilies, rose nor violet; the apple-tree bear flowers and fruit together on one bough. Youth and maiden live together in that place without blot or shame. Old age is unknown; there is neither sickness nor suffering—everything is full of joy. No one selfishly keeps anything to himself; here everything is shared.

In other cultures this would have been called an earthly paradise; to the Celts it was a place as simple and real as any that might be found in the realms of men. We may wonder at a realm where sickness and sorrow, old age and misery are banished; where men and women live together in peace and harmony, and where all things are provided from the goodness and plenty of the earth. To the Celtic storytellers who first told the stories of Arthur, such places lay no more than a heartbeat away.

It was perhaps inevitable, given the increase of Christian themes in the Arthurian stories, that something had to be found that would parallel the quest for the magical realms, and a love of the immortal women who lived there. The seeds were already there in the account of Arthur's voyage to the Otherworld in search of a magical vessel of immortality. From this emerged one of the most enduring strands of the entire Arthurian mythology, one that gave an alternative to the loves of Lancelot and Tristan, replacing them with spiritual love and longing. All this came to the fore in the last great development of the Arthurian story—the Quest for the Grail.

THE GREAT QUEST

OPPOSITE: Many chalices were said to be the actual Holy Grail used by Christ to celebrate the Last Supper. The fourteenth-century Bertinus Chalice, now kept in the New York Metropolitan Museum of Art, is one of the most famous.

There entered into the hall the Holy Grail, covered with white samite, that there was none might see it, nor who bare it. And then was the hall filled with good odours, and every knight had such meets and drinks as he loved best of this world.

SIR THOMAS MALORY: *LE MORTE D'ARTHUR*,
BOOK XIII. CHAPTER 9

THE ORIGINS OF THE GRAIL LEGENDS are no easier to define than the first accounts of Arthur. Many versions of the central story exist, and follow a similar pattern of development, from fragments discovered in Celtic literature and tradition down to the rich and complex romances of the Middle Ages. Whatever, ultimately, one thinks the Grail is, it is impossible not to recognize its importance within the framework of the Arthurian saga, while setting much of the story within the landscape of Britain melds it firmly to the mythic and heroic strands of the native tradition.

Despite claims for an even more primitive origin for the Grail, the earliest written references—just as for Arthur—derive from Celtic traditions. Before the Grail assumes the form with which we are most familiar—that of a cup or chalice—we find it in the shape of a cauldron. Celtic myth is full of references to such vessels, which are imbued with a variety of magical or miraculous qualities. There is, for example, the Cauldron of Inspiration or Awen, guarded by the Welsh corn and fertility goddess Ceridwen. Another is the Hamper or Basket of Gwydddno Garanhir, which had the quality that although only enough food was put into it for one person, enough could be taken out to feed a hundred. In other words the Grail at this stage is a container of plenty, an inexhaustible fund of good things—another of its later attributes.

But the most intriguing of these vessels of wonder is the Cauldron of Annwn. References to it abound in the earliest Celtic literature and traditions. The most interesting of these is a poem attributed to Taliesin,which has been dated to the ninth century. In fact it contains elements from a far earlier, oral tradition, and almost certainly dates back to the historical Arthur's time or even earlier. In the form that it has come down to us, Arthur is depicted as a heroic leader in search of the wondrous cauldron for himself. This makes it the earliest surviving text referring to such an adventure involving Arthur and his heroes—though it was certainly not to be the last. Although the language is at times obscure, it is nonetheless worth quoting in full:

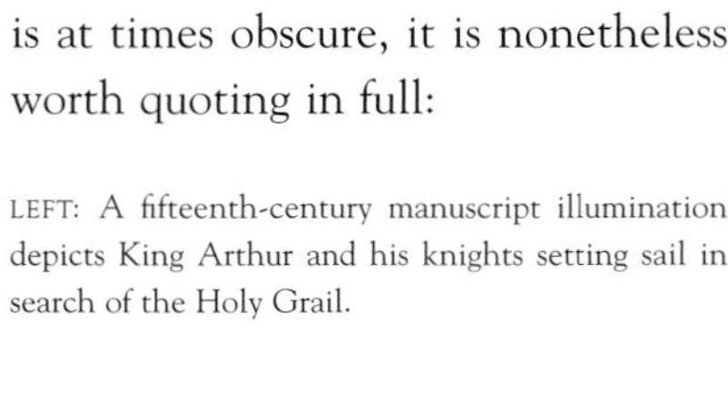

LEFT: A fifteenth-century manuscript illumination depicts King Arthur and his knights setting sail in search of the Holy Grail.

Prieddeu Annwn (Spoils of the In-World)

In Caer Siddi Gwair's prison was readied,
As Pwyll and Pryderi foretold,
None before went there save he,
Where the heavy chains bound him.
Before the spoiling of Annwn he sang forever
This eternal invocation of poets:
Save only seven, none returned from Caer Siddi.

Since my song resounded in the turning Caer,
I am pre-eminent. My first song
Was of the Cauldron itself.
Nine maidens kindled it with their breath –
Of what nature was it?
Pearls were about its rim,
it would not boil a coward's portion.
Lleminawg thrust his flashing sword
Deep within it;
And before dark gates, a light was lifted.
When we went with Arthur—a mighty labour—
Save only seven, none returned from Caer Fedwydd.

I am pre-eminent
Since my song resounded
In the four-square city,
In the Island of the Strong Door.
The light was dim and mixed with darkness,
Though bright wine was set before us.
Three shiploads of Prydwen went with Arthur –
Save only seven, none returned from Caer Rigor.

Worth more am I than the clerks
Who have not seen Arthur's might
Beyond Caer Siddi.
Six thousand stood on its walls—
It was hard to speak with their leader.
Three shiploads of Prydwen went with Arthur—
Save seven only, none returned from Caer Goludd.

I merit more than empty bards
Who know not the day, the hour or the moment
When the chick was born;
Who have not journeyed
To the courts of heaven;
Who know nothing of the meaning
Of the starry-collared ox
With seven score links in his collar.
When we went with Arthur—that sorrowful journey –
Save seven only, none returned from Manawyddan's Caer.

I know more forever than the weak-willed clerks
Who know not the day of the king's birth,
Nor the nature of the beast they guard for him.
When we went with Arthur—lamentable day—
Save only seven, none returned from Caer Achren.

(*Translated by the author*)

We are not told the names of the seven men who survived this mysterious voyage. Arthur is one, clearly; Taliesin himself—since he is telling the story—is another. The identities of the rest we can only guess at—though it is reasonable to suppose that Llwch Lleminawg (the original Lancelot) may be another, and possibly Bedwyr and Kai. Indeed, the whole story is really only hinted at. The Cauldron is tended by nine women—possibly priestesses—and their breath warms the vessel's rim. We know there are warriors to the tune of six thousand, led by a mysterious leader with whom it was hard to converse. We are told nothing about the Cauldron itself, or even whether the raid is successful. All we do know is that there are seven islands or cities to which the voyagers go in search of their prize, each of which contains a further test.

This is a pattern that is reflected in the later Grail romances, and implies a strong heritage of common elements in both. The

Before the Grail was linked with the Last Supper, older stories were told of the quest for the Cauldron of Rebirth. The Gundestrup Cauldron (above) may have fueled such stories.

Cauldron itself is here given no specific set of attributes beyond the fact that it will not boil food for a coward—an important factor among a people so utterly given over to personal bravery. These same qualities are inherited in enhanced form in the later medieval legends, where the Grail can only be won by the worthiest knight, and where it frequently provides the food most desired.

The Perfect Fool

Celtic tradition continued to be a powerful influence on the developing Grail mythology throughout the Middle Ages, and many of the primary themes within the later cycles of stories can be traced back to these early beginnings. However, the first written story of the Grail which is still extant makes it neither pagan nor Christian—though it is possible to interpret it either way.

Chrétien de Troyes, already famous for his poems on various aspects of the Arthurian tradition, began work on his final romance c. 1181. It was entitled *Perceval*, or *The Story of the Grail*. He died before finishing it, and left an enigma that has exercised the minds and haunted the dreams of countless seekers after wisdom ever since. The story he told may be summarized briefly as follows.

Perceval is brought up in the forest by his mother, who having lost a husband and three other sons in battle is determined that her remaining child shall know nothing of war or contest of arms. One day, Perceval encounters three of Arthur's knights, mistaking them at first for angels because of their shining armor, and learns

George Frederic Watts's nineteenth-century painting shows Sir Perceval, one of only three knights to succeed in the Quest for the Grail.

Julius Deitz's brooding picture of the Grail Castle. Here many tests and trials waited the knights in quest of the Holy Grail before those who survived were finally granted a vision of the vessel.

something of the world of men. From this moment on, Perceval decides that he must leave home in search of adventure. Despairing, his mother dresses him in shabby clothes, mounts him on a spavined horse, and arms him with a cooking-pot helmet and roughly fashioned spears, in the hope that his foolish appearance will prevent him from encountering any serious harm. She also tells him that if he should encounter any women on the way he should take a ring and a kiss from them, but nothing more.

Perceval's first encounter is with the Damsel of the Tent, who reacts somewhat adversely when he follows his mother's advice. Forced to flee from her jealous lover, Perceval nevertheless does not forget her. Arriving at Arthur's court he is in time to witness an insult to the Queen, in which a knight spills wine over her and steals her cup. Determining to take this as his first adventure Perceval sets out in pursuit of the knight, kills him, and is in the process of trying to boil the remains in order to obtain his adversary's armor, when he is discovered by an older knight named Govenal. This man becomes a father figure to the young Perceval, and trains him in the manners and mores of chivalry. Before they part he gives Perceval a second piece of advice, in addition to that of the boy's mother: never to speak out of turn or ask foolish questions for the sake of curiosity.

This advice affects Perceval's next adventure, in which he stumbles upon the Castle of the Grail. A fisherman, who eventually turns out to be Perceval's uncle, directs him there. Within the castle Perceval witnesses a mysterious procession, in which a candelabra, a spear that drips blood from the point, and a mysterious object called "a graal," are born through the hall. In an inner room lies an ancient man (the fisherman), who appears to be close to death, but is kept alive by food provided by the "graal."

None of this is explained and Perceval, mindful of Govenal's advice, forbears to ask its meaning. He goes to bed and next morning awakens to find himself lying on stones and the castle vanished. He is then challenged by a hideously ugly maiden, who accuses him of failing to take advantage of an opportunity for great good. Outcast and wretched, Perceval wanders for a long while in the wilderness, until he happens to meet a group of pilgrims. They remind him that it is Good Friday, when all good Christians should attend confession and celebrate the Eucharist.

ABOVE: A montage of scenes from the fifteenth-century *Roman de Tristan*, showing the Knights of the Round Table preparing to set forth in quest of the Grail.

Making his way to a hermitage in the forest, Perceval learns that his mother has died, grief-stricken, after he failed to return or send word of his adventures. Filled with remorse Perceval prepares to set out again in search of the mysterious castle of the fisherman. The story then turns to the adventures of Gawain, who is also in search of the Grail; but halfway through this part of the story, the narrative breaks off in mid-sentence, leaving everything unexplained.

So great was the power of the mystery evoked by this tale that other writers attempted to complete Chrétien's story. Long before they did so, however, other independent versions of the Grail story appeared. Robert de Boron wrote a trilogy of works in which he attempted to fill in the missing parts of Chrétien's story. His single greatest contribution to the legend was to identify the Grail with the Cup of the Last Supper, thus making the saga part of Christian tradition. This soon became a central strand in the evolving Grail saga and sparked off a succession of further narratives in which the story reached a level of detail and power probably undreamed of by either Chrétien or Robert.

Perceval was established as the Champion of the Grail, and stories of increasing complexity extended his role and attempted to explain the meaning of the sacred vessel in bewildering detail. New dimensions were added to the myth at every point. The Grail Guardian became one of a family of such people, descended from the Jewish Joseph of Arimathea, who gave up his own tomb to house the body of Christ and was said to have received the Grail—and its secret teachings—from the risen Messiah in person.

At some point in the development of the tales the ancient man in the castle becomes a king. His infirmity is explained as the result of a blow struck, either accidentally or as the retribution for some great wickedness, by a knight who is sometimes called Balin the Savage—viewed by some as symbol of paganism. This act became knows as "the Dolorous Blow," and not only did it cause an unhealing wound that could only be set right by the destined Grail winner, but it also laid

OPPOSITE: The ruins of the Castle of Dinas Bran in North Wales is believed by many people to be the original Castle of the Grail.

RIGHT: Sir Perceval, Sir Galahad and Sir Bors, the three knights who were destined to find the Grail. Galahad holds the sacred vessel while the others look on.

waste to the Kingdom of the Grail Family, which became a desert place in which the most terrible adventures and tests of the quest took place. This realm, known as "the Waste Land," would only be made whole when the Grail Knight came and asked a ritual question. This would set in motion a chain of events—the healing of the King, the fructification of the dead land, and something less tangible than either of these actions, which would somehow bring transformation to the whole world.

The Flowering of the Story

In the years that followed, the story of the Grail developed beyond the wildest imaginings of the storytellers who first shaped it. On to the scaffolding of Perceval's story was grafted a vast edifice of theological interpretation and commentary. Every nuance of the original story was examined, polished, changed and set in place like jewels in a complex setting. New characters, including the saintly knight Sir Galahad, who surpassed the original Grail winner and established a whole new branch of the mysteries, entered the story, which continued to expand with seemingly endless new adventures. Everyone, it seemed, wanted to know about Arthur and the Grail—and there was certainly no shortage of writers prepared to fulfil that desire.

But probably the most important of all these later versions is actually not one story but five separate—though interconnected—tales, which narrate the whole mighty saga of Arthur from birth to death, and include the Grail story in magnificent detail. Once attributed to a cleric named Walter Map, the cycle is now seen as the work of several hands—probably monks and clerics of the Cistercian order, founded by Saint Bernard of Clairvaux in 1115.

Galahad prepares himself for the final vision of the Grail. An image from a set of stamps illustrated by Yvonne Gilbert and issued by the UK Post Office in 1985.

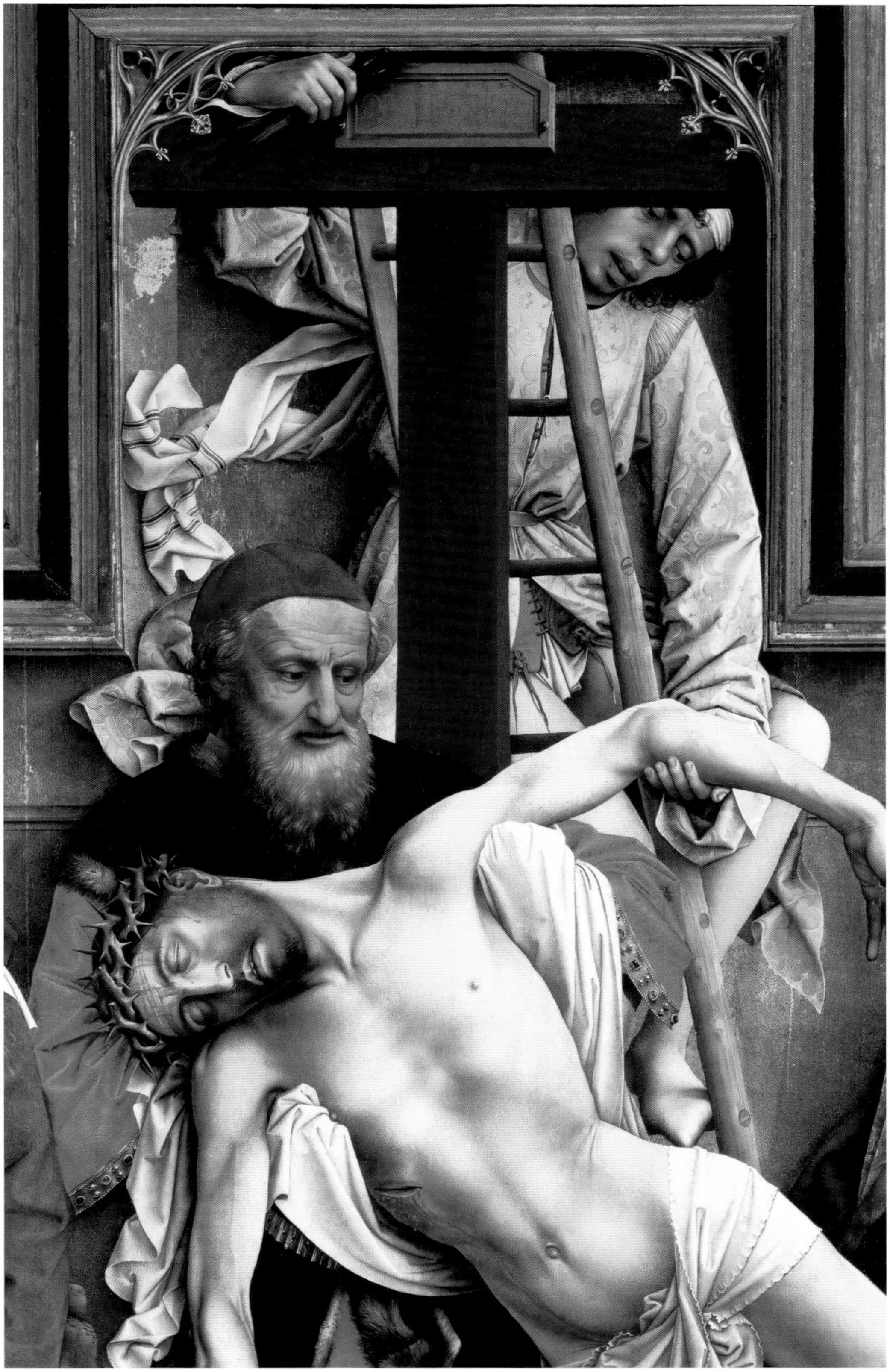

Detail from Roger van der Weyden's *Deposition* (c. 1435–8). Joseph of Arimathea cradles Christ's body.

The cycle marks the shift from tales composed largely in verse, to prose. The resulting elaboration of theme and style makes for heavy going today, and the stories have a tendency to be almost lost under a welter of theology. Nevertheless *The Vulgate Cycle* is in many ways a crowning achievement—the longest and most coherent of all the Arthurian romances.

The introduction states that the author, who wishes to remain anonymous, received a vision of Christ, who gave him a book that contained the history of the Holy Grail. Essentially, the story that follows is a thinly disguised excuse to explain the meaning of various doctrines—including the Trinity and the Incarnation—in mystical terms. It describes how Joseph of Arimathea was entrusted with the Cup of the Last Supper by Christ himself. After various adventures Joseph arrives in Britain, where he swiftly begins the task of converting the pagan inhabitants into Christians, founding various churches. When Joseph and his son Josephus finally die, a castle, called "Corbenic," is built to house the holy relics. The line of the Grail Kings is then described, several of whom are relatives of the later Arthurian characters—notably Lancelot and Gawain. One of the kings, Pelleam (who in some texts is called Pelles), receives a mysterious wound that will not heal, and is named "The Maimed King," the area around the castle of the Grail becomes the Waste Land—a dead place where no water flows and no trees or crops grow.

According to legend, Joseph of Arimathea brought the Holy Grail to a tiny church on the site of Glastonbury Abbey.

The Best Knight in the World

The third volume of the cycle concentrates on the history of Lancelot and prepares the way for the great quest to come. *The Vulgate Cycle*, which is sometimes known as *The Lancelot-Grail*, tells the story of the death of King Ban whose son, Lancelot, is stolen by the Lady of the Lake. Lancelot's childhood in the magical house beneath the water is described until, at the age of 15, he is ready to go forth into the world. The Lady takes him to Arthur and personally asks the king to bestow the accolade of knighthood upon her young charge. The innocent Lancelot meets Guinevere for the first time and is enraptured by her beauty. He embarks on a series of fantastic adventures and at length achieves the tests and trials of the castle named Dolorous Garde. He changes its name—to Joyous Garde—and makes the castle his home.

Lancelot continues to love Guinevere from afar and some time after happens by the Castle of the Grail—though he does not know it is this—where he is made welcome. He rescues Elaine, the daughter of the Grail King, from an enchanted cauldron, and on the night following is tricked into believing that he is sleeping with Guinevere. In fact he lies with Elaine, and Galahad is conceived, of whom it is predicted that he will surpass his father and win the Grail.

Signs and portents begin to appear everywhere in the Arthurian kingdom—the mysteries of the Grail are approaching. Guinevere, learning of Lancelot's unwitting liaison with Elaine, upbraids him for his faithlessness to her. Lancelot goes mad as a result and wanders in the forest for many months until he is finally rescued and healed by his cousin Bors.

At about his time Perceval, now 15, arrives at court and a hitherto mute damsel speaks and assigns him a seat at the Round Table next to the Siege Perilous—the seat that is destined to be occupied by the Grail winner himself. The child Galahad is put to school in a convent governed by the Fisher King's sister. This part of the cycle ends with the announcement that the Grail will appear at the next Whitsuntide.

This immensely long work is a staggering achievement in storytelling. Written in a style known as *entrelacement* (interlacing) it keeps several stories—sometimes as many as eight—going at once: beginning one, interrupting that with a second, interrupting that with a third, and so on, eventually returning to the first. This method not only challenges the reader to keep a great deal of information in his or her head, but makes for a good deal of suspense; often the author will stop an adventure at a real cliff-hanger, leaving the reader or listener to wait for fifty pages or so before the story is brought to a conclusion, or sometimes interrupted again.

The story of Lancelot is really a lengthy allegory about the strengths and weaknesses of

RIGHT: In this Nora Chesson illustration, Sir Lancelot gives his shield to Elaine before setting off in search of the Grail.

chivalry and earthly love compared to the power of spirituality and love for God. Lancelot is the strongest knight in the world but has a fatal flaw—he loves Arthur's queen. This will result in the eventual downfall of the Round Table and of Arthur's kingdom. One of the most extraordinary episodes in the entire Arthurian corpus is that in which Lancelot sleeps with Elaine. The outcome of this is the birth of Galahad, who will succeed in the Quest for the Grail. Thus out of the "sinful" love of Lancelot and Guinevere comes the most perfect spiritual knight ever to sit at the Round Table. This is a masterstroke that could only have been conceived by a storyteller of the highest order. His skill changed the face of the story forever.

The Glorious Quest

All is now in readiness for the coming of the Grail and all the wondrous events that were to follow. With the beginning of the next book, *The History of the Grail,* all the carefully laid threads of the story begin to come together, and the work moves toward its climax.

The story begins at Pentecost Eve. At Camelot writing appears on the Round Table to denote each knight's destined place, and announcing that the Siege Perilous will soon be filled. A floating stone appears in the river beside the palace, containing a sword that is destined to belong to the best knight. None is able to draw it out. During the meal, an ancient hermit enters

A fifteenth-century illumination from *The Vulgate Cycle* shows a hermit bringing the young Galahad to the Round Table.

bringing Galahad, and announces that the young knight will let loose enchantments that will blemish the land. Galahad sits in Siege Perilous, and his name appears on the table. He then pulls the sword from the floating stone and a maiden appears to present him with a shield.

The Grail now appears, as the knights are seated at supper:

> *When they were all seated in silence, there was heard such a great and marvellous peal of thunder that it seemed to them the palace must collapse. But at once there shone in upon them a ray of sunlight which made the palace seven-fold brighter than it was before. And straightway they were as if illumined with the grace of the Holy Spirit, and they began to look at one another; for they knew not whence this experience had befallen them ... Then ... there entered in the Holy Grail covered with a white cloth; but no one was able to see who was carrying it. It entered by the great door of the hall, and as soon as it had come in, the hall was filled with odours as sweet as if all the spices of the earth were defused there. And it passed down the middle of the hall and all around the high seats; and as it passed before the tables, they were straightway filled at each place with such viands as the occupant desired. When all were served the Holy Grail departed at once so that they knew not what had become of it nor did they see which way it went.*

Gawain vows to go in quest of the Grail at once and look upon its mystery openly. The rest of the knights promise to join him on the quest. Arthur declares this to be "a mortal blow" to him personally, for he will lose his great Fellowship of Knights. The ladies wish to accompany the knights, but are forbidden by a hermit:

LEFT: The quest knights take leave of their ladies in this modern stained glass.

ABOVE AND RIGHT: St Goven's Chapel in Cornwall was, according to local tradition, the place where the Quest for the Grail began. The knights came here for a blessing before setting forth.

"For this is no search for earthly things, but a seeking out of the mysteries and hidden sweets of Our Lord." Arthur bids farewell to his knights; Guinevere takes her leave of Lancelot; the knights go their separate ways.

The story now follows the adventures of the main knights—those of Galahad, Lancelot and Gawain taking up most of the space. Gawain encounters a hermit who tells him roundly that he will not succeed and explains graphically why: he is too much in love with the world, and beautiful women, to aspire to the heights of spiritual honor. Lancelot rests near a mysterious deserted chapel where candles are still burning and sees a sick knight in a litter, though he does not greet him. The man laments that he shall never see the Holy Vessel. It appears on a silver table. The sick knight prays to it and is healed, but falls asleep instantly. The Grail returns to the chapel without Lancelot noticing. A squire returns to dress the healed knight, and steals Lancelot's armor and his horse. Lancelot awakes as from a dream and enters the chapel to seek the Grail. He is told: "Lancelot, harder than stone, more bitter than wood, more barren and bare than the fig tree, how … do you dare enter where the Grail is?" Lancelot laments and comes to a hermitage where he makes confession. Able at last to unburden himself of the sinful love of Guinevere, Lancelot is absolved and given new arms and rehorsed.

Perceval finds his way to the cell of an anchoress who is also his aunt. She dissuades him from trying to better Galahad and tells him that he, Galahad and Bors are destined to find the Grail. She tells him that she was once Queen of the Waste Land and that his mother died of sorrow at his leaving. She also foretells that just as the Gospel of Christ was made manifest at Pentecost, so will the mysteries of the Grail. The anchoress then bids Perceval travel to Corbenic, the castle of the Grail. As he travels on close to the sea, he sees a boat coming toward him impelled by the wind. The beautiful maiden of the boat tells him of Galahad's adventures, and bids him accompany her. She sets up a tent to shelter them both, then feeds Perceval, who in turn woos her. As he is lying in bed waiting for her his gaze falls upon the cross hilt of his sword and remembers his quest. The tent vanishes and Perceval wounds himself in the thigh in penance. A priest appears and prepares to lead him to Bors and Galahad.

The story now turns to Bors, Lancelot's cousin. He meets a maiden who desires him. When he rejects her, she threatens to leap with 12 of her maidens from the tower. Bors refuses her and she jumps. The tower and maidens disappear and fiendish shrieks are heard. Bors hears a voice that bids him find the sea and Perceval. He finds Perceval on a boat with white sails. They tell each other of their adventures.

While staying at a hermitage, Galahad is called to follow a maiden who conducts him to the ship where Bors and Perceval are. The maiden says she is Perceval's sister, Dindraine. They see a canopied bed with a crown and scabberdless sword upon it.

Parsifal in Quest of the Holy Grail, by Ferdinand Leeke, shows the knight setting forth. He carries the shield of the Knights Templar.

Dindraine explains the history of the sword: how the ship came to Britain in the time of Lambar, the father of the present Maimed King, and how the pagan King Varlan drew the sword and used it to wound Lambar. This was the first dolorous blow. The sword belt proclaims it may not be unfastened save by the hand of princess who will exchange it for a worthy belt, and that the maiden shall truly name the sword. The framework over the bed is made of the white, red and green woods that originated in the Garden of Eden.

Dindraine weaves a belt from her hair and names the sword "Memory of Blood." Galahad takes it and they get into their own ship and sail onward. Later they are stopped, Dindraine is captured and a leprous maiden seeks to be healed by her blood. After Mass, Dindraine is bled, but the bleeding will not stop and she begins to die. She bids Perceval and Galahad put her in a boat and travel to Sarras, the holy city of the Grail, where they will find her.

Meanwhile, Lancelot finds himself hemmed in by a dark forest, high rocks and deep rivers. He enters a boat without oar or sail, sleeps and on waking sees Dindraine's body. He reads a letter placed there by Perceval. At last he meets Galahad and they stay on board the boat—the Ship of Solomon—for six months. During this time they grow to know and love each other and share many adventures. Then at Easter, they meet a hermit with a horse who bids Galahad carry on his quest.

After a month alone at sea, Lancelot comes to a castle guarded by two lions. He draws his sword and is transfixed by a flaming hand. He enters the chapel of the Grail and rushes forward to help support the priest, whom he perceives as holding up the body of a crucified man. He is paralyzed and blinded for daring to enter the holy place. Slowly he is nursed back to health and finds that he is at Corbenic. Lancelot comes to table that is set by the Grail but afterward departs to return to Camelot.

Galahad, Perceval, and Bors wander for a further five years. They come to Corbenic and Pelles greets his grandson, Galahad.

The sword, with which Joseph of Arimathea was wounded in the thigh, is brought in, broken. Galahad unites it and a voice bids all unclean persons avoid the hall. Newcomers arrive from other countries and a bed is borne in by four maidens. All leave save the Grail companions. The Maimed King is on the bed. Josephus, the first Christian bishop of Britain, mysteriously appears and the holy things manifest in the hall. Christ appears from the Grail and gives it to each one of the knights to drink. Galahad anoints the Maimed King with blood from the lance, healing him. They find the Ship of Solomon again, and the Grail appears on it. They set sail and arrive at Sarras and take the Grail into the city. Galahad is made king of Sarras. After a year he looks into the Grail and dies. Perceval and Bors see a hand snatch up the Grail to heaven. Perceval becomes a hermit and Bors stays for a year until he dies, then returns to Logres (the ancient name for Arthur's Britain) and tells Arthur all that has occurred.

Thus ends this great and magisterial account. Despite its great length, prolixity and extensive theological argument it is a truly powerful and at times awe-inspiring romance. Few can fail to be moved by the story of Lancelot, his all-too-human struggle to overcome his mortal love and achieve the spiritual mystery. Perceval and Bors seem shadowy by comparison, and certainly Perceval is a less important figure than Galahad. It is Lancelot's son who holds center stage throughout most of the romance—dominating it with his saintly presence. He has been described as a cold and bloodless hero, but in truth he is a simple and godly man who bears the task for which he has been born with strength and honor. The months he spends with his father on the Ship of Solomon are filled with moving moments as the relationship between father and son grows and develops. In the end both are ennobled—Lancelot by his son's extraordinary purity of mind, and Galahad by his father's stubborn worldliness.

Galahad in Solomon's Ship, by Edwin Austin Abbey (1895). The mysterious vessel carries the Grail knight to the Holy city of Sarras where the Grail will finally rest.

The final celebration of the Mass of the Grail is celebrated by Joseph of Arimathea himself, surrounded by angels. Galahad looks on in wonder in this painting by Edwin Austin Abbey.

The Last Great Telling

There were still many retellings of the Grail story to follow, but none of them added significantly to the tale as it had been told by Chrétien and elaborated in *The Vulgate Cycle*. In the fifteenth century Sir Thomas Malory took the mighty saga and turned it into one of the greatest books ever written in the English language—*Le Morte D'Arthur*. He cut the text by more than half, jettisoned the theological arguments and courtly descriptions, and replaced them with realistic dialogue and a fast-moving narrative style that make the book as much of a joy to read to this day.

Malory's book is memorable for many reasons—its sense of character, style and the sheer gift of the storyteller have seldom been equaled. He makes the Grail even more mysterious than it is in *The Vulgate Cycle*, explaining very little and embellishing so deftly that one is left gasping in admiration at his subtlety. But *Le Morte D'Arthur* could not have been written without the existence of *The Vulgate*, which is still the most complete retelling of the stories ever attempted. It may lack for pace to our modern senses, but it more than makes up for this in the sheer inventiveness and richness of the stories, which tumble on, like a vast unstoppable river, for hundreds of pages.

Throughout the remainder of the Middle Ages the Arthurian saga continued to be the most popular subject for writers in the Europe. Countless authors added to it, duplicating, contradicting each other, elaborating on theme after theme. The story of Arthur had come a long way from the fragmentary chronicles of the sixth and seventh centuries and the pseudo-history of Geoffrey of Monmouth. Yet no matter how complex and detailed the retellings became, it was still possible to see the bones of Geoffrey's *Historia Regum Brittaniae*, and even a distant echo of the heroic leader who fought off the Saxons and in so doing wrote himself a page in one of the most vivid eras in British history.

Toward the end of the Middle Ages interest in the Arthurian legends began to wane. No lesser person than the poet John Milton toyed with the idea of writing an epic of Arthur, but chose the Biblical theme of The Fall instead, the result of which was *Paradise Lost* (1667). The period from the sixteenth to the eighteenth centuries saw few new versions of the stories and few even believed in the existence of a historical Arthur. But the nineteenth century was to see an explosion of interest that has continued unabated ever since. The long and complex history of Arthur was about to find fresh soil, from which would spring countless new shoots. The final chapter in Arthur's story, which brings it up to date, leads us into territory both old and new—back into the mists of Celtic history and forward to the distant future.

7 THE ONCE AND FUTURE KING

OPPOSITE: Arthur (Clive Owen) is a Romano-British war leader in Jerry Bruckheimer's movie *King Arthur* (2004) based on Marion Zimmer Bradley's best-selling novel.

Yet some men say in many parts of England that King Arthur is not dead, but had by the will of Our Lord Jesu into another place; and men say that he shall come again ... I will not say it shall be so, but rather will I say: here in this world he changed his life.

SIR THOMAS MALORY: *LE MORTE D'ARTHUR*

A Mutable Image

FROM THE EARLIEST TIMES the Arthurian tradition has been subject to constant, often subtle degrees of change. The heroic mold that gave us the earliest figure of Arthur gave way to that of the mythic dimension, before becoming the chivalric king ruling over an elegant medieval court. Later ages presented him within a more political framework, with spurious prophecies—attributed to Merlin—declaring for the latest regime. Both the Plantaganets and the Tudors leant heavily on the presence of Arthur in their family trees to uphold their claims to the throne of Britain. Henry II, the first of the Plantagenet kings, did his best to prove that Arthur was indeed dead and not about to return and restore the line of native British kings, while at the same time claiming a dynastic link with the great king to support his own place on the throne. This certainly accounts for his interest in the discovery of Arthur's bones in 1191 at Glastonbury Abbey in Somerset.

The story is interesting not only for this reason, but for the light it throws on how Arthur was viewed during his period of history. It is said that Henry received information from a certain Breton storyteller of the whereabouts of Arthur's grave, and that a subsequent excavation in the abbey cemetery unearthed a massive coffin, made from a single hollowed-out tree. Within this were some "gigantic" bones and a lead cross on which was inscribed the words:

HIC JACET SEPULTUS INCLITUS REX
ARTHURI IN INSULA AVALONIA

(Here lies buried the famous king Arthur in the Isle of Avalon.)

The effect of this discovery was to turn Glastonbury into an instant pilgrimage site, with hundreds of people coming to stare at Arthur's grave. This certainly did the fortunes of the abbey no harm, as they had suffered a disastrous fire shortly before and now received a grant from the crown to rebuild. For the Plantaganets it gave them a connection with a British "king" who was even more prestigious than Charlemagne, from whom their French rivals claimed descent. Nor would it seem to be an accident that Henry's son, Geoffrey, named his son Arthur, perhaps in the hope of reestablishing the Arthurian dynasty. If this was his intention it was to be foiled by the death of the 16-year-old Prince Arthur at the hands of his uncle, who became King John.

RIGHT: The wounded Arthur is carried to Avalon, watched over by three queens and their women in this nineteenth-century woodcut.

ELISABETHA
REG: ANGLIÆ.

The site of Arthur's grave is still a source of debate, like so much else of Arthur's story. Many historians believe it to have been a hoax perpetrated by the Glastonbury monks; however, modern archaeology has indicated that the site was indeed excavated in the twelfth century and that the inscription on the lead cross was much older than this period—though probably not as old as the sixth century. Since both the bones and the lead cross have been missing since the sixteenth century nothing can be proved either way.

Edward I (*reigned* 1272–1307) certainly believed the story. He had the bones transferred to a magnificent black marble tomb in front of the High Altar in the Abbey Church in 1278. Edward III (*reigned* 1327–77) was also something of an Arthurian fanatic, visiting Glastonbury on a number of occasions, collecting Arthurian texts and dressing in clothes embroidered with images from the Tristan stories. In 1334 he proposed the restoration of the Fellowship of the Round Table, and though this became the Order of the Garter, he used the idea of Arthur's knights as a basis for his chivalric dreams. He encouraged the organization of pageants known as "Round Tables" and may well have ordered the construction of the table that now hangs in the Great Hall at Winchester—though this was later repainted to show Henry VIII in the guise of Arthur.

Edward IV, who came to the throne in 1461, was equally fascinated by the stories of the legendary monarch. Prophecies current at the time of his birth and childhood had pointed to the coming of truly great king, cast in the mold of Arthur, and many regarded Edward quite literally as Arthur returned. Edward was sufficiently convinced by this to employ researchers to draw up elaborate family trees and horoscopes that proved beyond a doubt that he was descended from Arthur. His death in 1483 dashed the hopes of many people who believed that the great king had returned. In the succeeding years, with the regency of the king's younger brother, Richard Duke of Gloucester (who briefly reigned as Richard III), the suspicious death of Edward's son, and the following scramble for power it must have seemed as though the dream of a restored Arthurian kingdom was dead forever.

But with the ending of the Plantaganet line at the Battle of Bosworth Field in 1485 a new dynasty came to power: the Tudors, who were equally determined to prove their right to the kingdom by claiming descent from its premier king. Henry VII (*reigned* 1485–1509) supported his claim to the English throne by proving his descent from Cadwalleder, who according to Geoffrey of Monmouth was the last of the British kings, and through him from Arthur himself. To emphasize this still further Henry saw to it that his wife Elizabeth was confined at Winchester for the birth of their first child. There, in the city believed by many to be the site of Camelot, the queen gave birth to a son, who was promptly christened Arthur with the express wish that "there might be another king of that name in Britain."

OPPOSITE: For many people during her reign, Queen Elizabeth I was seen as a living representative of the line of Arthur. Many plays and pageants depicting Arthurian themes were performed at this time.

Unfortunately for Henry, the young prince proved as ill-fated as the other prince Arthur, and died in 1502, leaving his younger brother, Henry, to become king. Henry VIII (*reigned* 1509–47) was to transform England forever, and, like his ancestors, he continued to uphold the idea that his line descended from Arthur. In 1511 he spent over £4,000 (a considerable sum in those days) to organize a huge tournament at Winchester, in which he himself took part dressed as Arthur. The event was intended to celebrate the birth of a son, the third prince to bear the name Arthur, but the infant lived for only 52 days.

A few years later, when he faced King Francis I of France at the Field of the Cloth of Gold, Henry's banners depicted Arthur as conqueror of the world—the implication being that Henry could lay claim to lands all over Europe if he so chose. In 1522 Henry commissioned the repainting of the famous *Round Table* at Winchester so that it depicted him as a splendid King Arthur surrounded by his greatest knights. Both Henry and his daughter Elizabeth I cited early Arthurian chronicles in legal documents relating to their use of the term "Imperial Crown."

Thomas Churchyard, writing in his book *The Worthiness of Wales* in 1587, referred to the Elizabeth as:

She that sits in regall Throne,
With Sceptre, Sword, and Crowne.
(Who came from Arthur's rase and lyne).

Although Elizabeth never emphasized her own connections to Arthur, she certainly loved the stories. On one occasion, while on one of her famous progresses through the country, she attended a pageant at Kenilworth Castle in which her lover Robert Dudley played Arthur and which told the story of his love for the Lady of the Lake.

Still later, in 1610, the playwright Ben Jonson wrote a pageant called *The Speeches at Prince Henry's Barriers* in which he described Elizabeth's cousin, James I, as the monarch who, "wise, temperate, just, and stout, claims Arthur's seat." This was a reference to a popular anagram then circulating, which was designed to bolster the belief in James as the rightful king of Britain as well as Scotland, and which declared that:

Charles James Steuart
CLAIMES ARTHURS SEATE
referring to the great crag of this name that rises above the city of Edinburgh.

On the literary horizon, Arthur's star waned for a time. Spenser devoted the first part of his epic, *The Faerie Queen*, to the deeds of young Prince Arthur, and clearly drew upon Malory and earlier sources for his inspiration, but made no attempt to carry the story forward into the later part of the tales. Merlin made a brief appearance in 1605 in the story of *Don Quixote* by Miguel de Cervantes, and later still the visionary poet and painter, William Blake, referred to Arthur and Merlin in one of his most important works, *The Prophetic Books*. However, these were minor references that did no more than keep the names of the great heroes alive.

Then, in the nineteenth century, came the birth of Romanticism, and with this the figures of Arthur, Guinevere, Lancelot and Tristan underwent a renaissance. The poet laureate, Alfred Tennyson, wrote a cycle of long poems, *The Idylls of the King,* whose sonorous rhythms brought back something of the original power of the romances. However, Tennyson gave the knights Victorian values and all but dressed Arthur in a frock coat and stove-pipe hat!

Queen Victoria (*reigned* 1837–1901) herself, though claiming no specific dynastic descent from Arthur, loved Tennyson's poetry and was more than happy to endorse the mythic side of the story. She commissioned several painters to portray the Prince Consort as Arthur, while Albert himself had the artist William Dyce decorate the robing room at Westminster Palace with scenes from the Arthurian epic. The royal couple's third son was christened Arthur, though he never came to the throne.

Throughout the Victorian era, Arthurian themes dominated the arts of poetry, music and painting. The Pre-Raphaelite

A souvenir program from the nineteenth-century play *King Arthur* by J. Comyns Carr, which starred the great Henry Irving as Merlin.

Brotherhood, whose numbers included Dante Gabriel Rossetti, Edward Burne-Jones and William Morris, produced striking paintings based on Arthurian themes. One of the earliest photographers, Julia Margaret Cameron, produced a series of portraits of scenes from Tennyson's poems in which well-known people posed as Arthurian characters. Poetry, good, bad and indifferent, imitating Tennyson, poured forth and was avidly read. Plays and pageants were performed all over the country depicting the adventures of Arthur and his knights. The magic and beauty of the stories wove a spell over the drab Victorian age, touching again and again on the deepest levels of human experience.

A New Beginning

With the dawning of the twentieth century came war and destruction on a scale scarcely imagined before. A new breed of artists began to emerge, and among them were many who turned again to the images and stories of the Arthurian tradition for inspiration.

The poet and painter David Jones was one of these. He painted a number of extraordinary pictures on Arthurian themes—picturing the Grail Mass taking place in a bombed-out chapel in the middle of the new Waste Land of the Western Front, where he himself had fought. In his great poem *In Parenthesis,* he portrayed First World War soldiers fighting side by side with Arthurian heroes. In the work that followed it, *The Anathemata,* he produced an extraordinary evocation of Britain from its geological past to a semi-mythic eternity, bringing in the themes of Arthur and the Grail with tremendous force and vitality.

Modern techniques of archaeology, along with detailed research into the sparse documents of the sixth and seventh centuries, began to reveal more of the reality behind the earliest heroic tales. Archaeologists led the search for the truth about Arthur, excavating an Iron-Age camp at Cadbury in Somerset in the belief that it might be the original Camelot, and searched the ruins of the medieval castle at Tintagel in Cornwall for clues to Arthur's birth. The so-called Dark Ages were no longer so dark, and with this ever-widening pool of knowledge to draw upon, once again novelists and poets looked to the Arthurian tradition for their inspiration.

A number of memorable historical novels that drew on the Arthurian legend appeared from the 1940s onward. Edward Frankland wrote a detailed and poetic account of the historical Arthur in his book *The Bear of Britain*, and this was followed by such works as *The Great Captains* by Henry Treece, which told the story from the viewpoint of Mordred; *Porius* by John Cowper Powys, a vast sprawling romance worthy of the best of its medieval forbears but wholly contemporary; and perhaps best of all, *The Sword at Sunset* (1961) by Rosemary Sutcliff, which evoked a totally human Arthur, touched with the magic of a forgotten age, tragic and noble, still striving toward the ideal kingdom dreamed of in Malory's *Le Morte D'Arthur* and *The Vulgate Cycle.*

In the 1950s T.H. White published a quartet of books under the overall title *of The Once and Future King*, taking the Latin epitaph said to be carved upon the tomb where Arthur's bones were thought to have lain. In this he set out to tell the story as Malory had given it, but with a modern spin. The first book, *The Sword in the Stone*, tells the story of Arthur's childhood and training at the hands of Merlin—or rather, as White spells it, Merlyn. This rather comical old gentleman, who lives backward and is thus enabled to see the future which, to him, has already happened, seems a far cry from the Merlin of earlier times. Yet his magic is no less potent. Arthur learns the things that he needs to fit him for the great task ahead by taking the shapes of bird, beast and insect, each of which shows him the foolishness of the ways of men.

This light-hearted beginning became gradually darkened in the books that followed. *The Queen of Air and Darkness* concentrated on the figure of Morgause and the childhood of her sons Gawain, Gareth, Gaheries and Agravaine, and culminates in the birth of Mordred, whose coming is to spell destruction for the Arthurian world. The third in the series, *The Ill-Made Knight*, told the story of Lancelot and Guinevere with a degree of passion and psychological realism seldom attained before or since. Finally, *The Candle in the Wind* told the story of the downfall of the Round Table, the war against Lancelot and the doom-laden ending of the tale. A fifth volume, left unfinished by White at his death, was published later as *The Story of Merlyn.* It tells what happens when the old wizard returns to Arthur's tent on the eve of the Battle of Camlan, as he takes his protégé through a further series of transformations that equip him for a new beginning after his time in Avalon. It is marred by White's bitter response to the imminent war with Germany, but it nevertheless contains some of his finest writing, taking Arthur beyond the darkness in which his dream ends, toward a new source of light.

Poets did not neglect the tradition either. Following in Tennyson's footsteps, another poet laureate, John Masefield, produced a series of powerful lyrics in *Midsummer Night* mingling the heroic and the romantic elements of the old stories in a wholly new way. In the late 1930s and early 1940s, Charles Williams, one of the august group of intellectuals known as the

Inklings, who included J. R. R. Tolkien and C. S. Lewis among their number, wrote what is still the most powerful and magical series of poems on the theme of the Grail. He created an entire world, stretching from the negative realm of P'o L'u, to the great city of the Grail at Sarras. No simple account can give any real idea of the magisterial quality of these poems, which appeared in two volumes *Taliesin through Logres* and *The Region of the Summer Stars*.

In one poem Merlin and his twin sister, here called Brisen, who symbolize time and space in Williams's universe, and are the offspring of Nimue (who here represents nature), enact a magical operation to assist in the founding of the Arthurian kingdom.

The cone's shadow of earth fell into space,
and into (other than space) the third heaven.
In the third heaven are the living unriven truths,
climax tranquil in Venus. Merlin and Brisen
heard, as in faint bee-like humming
round the cone's point, the feeling intellect hasten
to fasten on the earth's image; in the third heaven
the stones of the waste glimmered like summer stars.
Between wood and waste the yoked children of Nimue
opened the rite; they invoked the third heaven,
heard in the far humming of the spiritual intellect,
to the building of Logres and the coming of the land of the Trinity,
which is called Sarras in maps of the soul. Merlin made preparation . . .
He lifted the five times cross-incised rod
and began incantation; in the tongue of Broceliande
adjuring all the primal atoms of earth
to shape the borders of Logres, to the dispensation
of Carbonek to Caerleon, of Caerleon to Camelot, to the union
of King Pelles and King Arthur . . .

Another distinguished poet, John Heath Stubbs, gave his vision of Arthur in a wide-ranging epic entitled *Artorius*, combining myth, romance, and the heroic in a subtle blend. More recently still there have been a positive spate of novels, many of which have looked back toward the Dark Ages for inspiration. Magic and mystery, druidcraft and wizardry dominate the pages of books like *The Mists of Avalon* by Marion Zimmer Bradley, which was subsequently filmed for television; *Down the Long Wind* by Gillian Bradshaw, and the trilogy of Merlin novels by Mary Stewart. Bradley tells her story from the viewpoint of Morgan le Fay, evoking a rich vision of Avalon as a fairy world, gradually floating away from the historical realm of Arthur. The same author also invokes the shadow of Atlantis in the early part of the book, making Arthur's mother Igrain one of the few who escaped (along with Merlin) from the drowned continent, bringing with her the bloodline and magical knowledge of the most ancient and advanced civilization on earth.

In her series of books about Gawain, Gillian Bradshaw again introduces magical themes into the narrative, giving to her hero the task of finding and wielding the magical sword of light under the aegis of the God Lugh. In doing so she harks back to a tradition which made Gawain the wielder of Excalibur, gifted to him by Arthur for a time in the wars against the Saxons.

The Merlin of Mary Stewart's trilogy is, as we have seen, more of a modern magician than the visionary and seer of earlier texts. Yet he is still a recognizable descendant of the Merlin Ambrosius written about by Geoffrey of Monmouth. He falls into inspired trances, and suffers the terrible agonies of the gifted psychic who sees all, but is helpless to do more than watch as the kingdom he helped to create falls back into the darkness from which it emerged.

Another book that borrows from Arthurian legend is *Corbenic* by Katherine Fisher. This tells a modern account of the Grail quest as it takes place in the life of a contemporary teenager named Cal whose experiences mirror those of Perceval. This powerful book re-creates the magic and mystery of the Arthurian world in terms that we can all relate to.

Visions of the Grail

The Grail indeed has had its share of the revival. A veritable industry of modern works have appeared in recent years, spinning out of the bright strands of Arthurian lore dozens of different theories regarding the origins, purpose and hiding place of this sacred relic.

Beginning in 1982 with the bestselling *Holy Blood, Holy Grail*, which put forward the astonishing theory that Jesus had married Mary Magdalen and sired the line of the Merovingian kings of France—with Magdalen herself the bearer of the bloodline of the Grail Kings—a new generation of researchers has sprung up, each with a theory to present. Theories relating to the medieval Order of the Knights Templars, who were rooted out and destroyed in the twelfth century for practicing "heretical" beliefs, state that they possessed the secret of the Grail. Another group, the Cathars, an obscure sect that sprang up in the south of France in the eleventh century, are likewise believed to have carried the Grail with them and to have hidden it in caves beneath a rocky outcrop called Montségur in the Pyrenees. So strong was this belief that

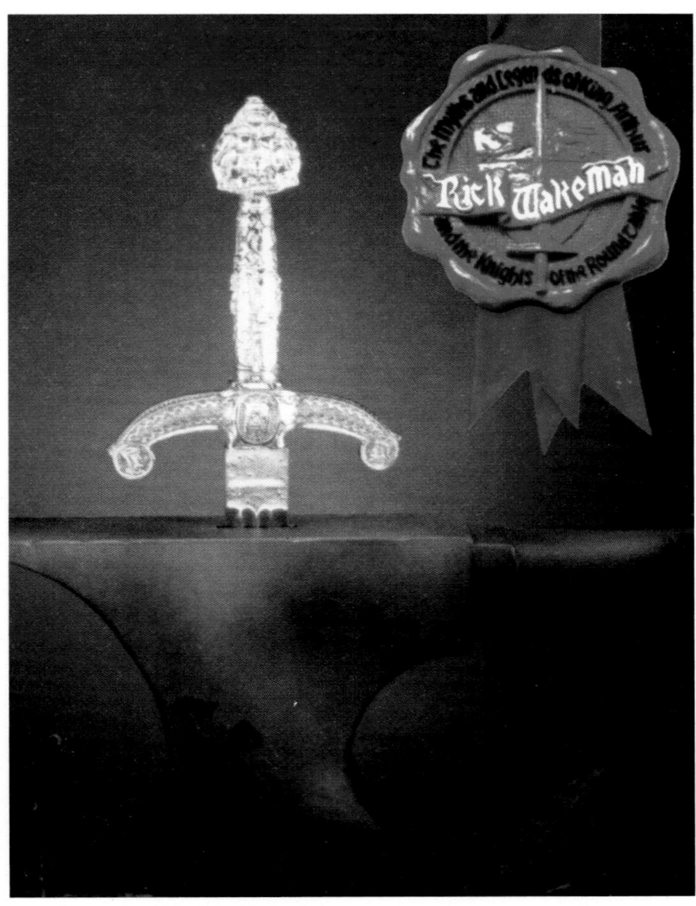

Cover image from Rick Wakeman's hugely successful rock album *The Myths and Legends of King Arthur and the Knights of the Round Table*.

Joseph Cipolla as Merlin and David Justin as Uther Pendragon in the 2001 production of David Bintley's ballet *Arthur* by the Birmingham Royal Ballet.

the Nazis sent men to dig in the caves during the Second World War in the hope of discovering the most scared and powerful relic in Christendom—a story that later resurfaced in the 1989 movie *Indiana Jones and the Last Crusade*.

Others have suggested various hiding places for the actual Grail, ranging from a remarkable chapel at Rosslyn, in Scotland, which possesses an intricate puzzle in stone carved on its walls, to a chalice kept in a glass case in the Metropolitan Museum of Art in New York.

Still another theory, which again connects the Templars with the Grail, has been put forward by Noel Currer-Briggs in a book called *The Shroud and the Grail*. This is a skillful piece of detective work which, convincingly enough, traces the ownership of the Holy Shroud, with which Christ's body was wrapped and which is said to bear his image impressed upon it, from the Holy Land to the city of Turin where it now resides.

The keys to the whereabouts of this most holy relic, particularly between 1204 and 1350, have been plausibly charted by Currer-Briggs to the Templars. He has identified the Shroud, folded so that only the image of the face was visible, both with another wonder-working image of Christ, the Mandilion, and with the infamous "Head," which heresy-hunters ascribed to the Templars as an idol that they were believed to worship.

Taking this as a starting point Currer-Briggs turns his attention to the Grail texts, which describe light emanating from the vessel and the form of a child within it. He then suggests that the word "Grail," subject to so many different interpretations and meanings, actually refers to the "grill" with which the Mandilion (in reality the folded Shroud) was covered or framed. Thus one could indeed be said to "look into" the Grail and see the form of Christ, or even a holy radiance, as Galahad is said to do in *The Vulgate Cycle*.

Whatever one ultimately thinks of all these theories—and there are many more that are far less probable than the ones mentioned here—the continuing interest in this aspect of the Arthurian tradition helps keep alive the subject as a whole.

Arthur on the Silver Screen

Contemporary cinema likewise has not neglected the realms of Arthur. At least one recent work, *Excalibur* (1981), directed by John Boorman, and cowritten with Rospo Pallenburg, gives a marvellously rich account of the whole cycle from Arthur's birth to his last battle. Though compressed at times to a point where it is difficult to comprehend, the subtext of the film has a unity rare in any Arthurian work. It makes significant use of the symbolism of the Grail Quest, and successfully demonstrates the links between Arthur and the Maimed King who, in this version, are one and the same. It also contains the best portrayal (by Nicol Williamson) of Merlin to date, as a wise, quirky, sorrowful figure who is the last Dragon Priest of Britain and draws upon the immense power of the earth to bring about his magical operations.

The latest, and perhaps the most exciting movie version of the Arthurian legends yet to emerge from Hollywood, takes us back to the fifth century, to a group of Sarmatian knights stationed on Hadrian's Wall and led by the charismatic Artorius Castus, a descendent of the original leader of Sarmatian warriors imported in Britain by the Emperor Hadrian (see Chapter One). *King Arthur* (2004), produced by Jerry Bruckheimer, directed by Antoine Fuqua, and written by David Franzoni, at last gives us an authentic story of the Dark-Age Arthur, stripped of magic and medieval romanticism and shown in all its bare, powerful savagery. Clive Owen makes a strong and thoughtful Arthur, and the rising British star Kiera Knightly, plays Guinevere, here a Pictish princess. Once again

ABOVE: Robert Taylor as Lancelot in the 1953 movie *Knights of the Round Table,* directed by Richard Thorpe.

RIGHT: Richard Harris as King Arthur, Venessa Redgrave as Guinevere and Franco Nero as Lancelot in the lavish movie version of Lerner & Loewe's musical *Camelot* (1967).

the struggle between the Romano-British and the invading Saxons is played out against the background of a stark Northern landscape. After decades of films portraying Arthur as a hero of medieval splendor, this movie points the way toward a revisioning of the character in more authentic terms.

Television also has had its share of Arthurian series and associations. The original series of *Star Trek* (1966–1969) told of the adventures of a band of latter-day knights under the leadership of a futuristic Arthur in the guise of the impulsive Captain James Tiberius Kirk, assisted by the very Merlinesque Mr. Spock. More recently *Babylon 5* (1993–1998), a dramatic space opera created by Michael J. Straczynski, has drawn heavily on the myths of Arthur.

Apparently, the Quest for the Grail is still continuing in the twenty-second century, as we learn in the episode entitled "Grail," written by Christy Marx. In this a wanderer named Aldous Gajic arrives on the *Babylon 5* space station. He describes himself as belonging to an "Order" though it is given no name, and he is in search of the Holy Grail, which he describes as "a sacred vessel of regeneration," also known as "The Cup of the Goddess."

The reaction of the humans on the station to Aldous's quest is somewhat negative: to them, the Grail is "just a myth." To the Minbari, a race of aliens who share the station, Aldous is an "honored seeker" who deserves proper acknowledgement. "It doesn't matter that this Grail may or may not exist," is their position, "but that [Aldous] strives for the perfection of his soul . . . and that he has never wavered or lost faith." This is really a very good description of the purpose of the Grail Quest, which is not a search for a lost treasure, but a journey in search of spiritual perfection.

The first thing that happens to Aldous is his meeting with Thomas Jordan, a simple man who resembles Perceval more than anyone. In fact there are a number of interesting echoes in the relationship of the two men, which resembles that between Galahad and Perceval. Aldous, like Galahad, dies when he finally sees the Grail. The passing on of the guardianship of the Grail from Galahad to Perceval is clearly echoed when the dying Aldous formally asks the station commander to witness that Thomas is his heir.

The Grail itself is seen as something miraculous, something

Sir Alec Guinness in the role of Obi-Wan Kenobi from the movie *Star Wars: A New Hope* (1977) directed by George Lucas. The character showed aspects of both knightly heroes and the wizardry of Merlin.

The TV series *Star Trek* (1966–1969) shows the influence of Arthurian stories in the Merlin-like figure of Mr. Spock (Leonard Nimoy) and the kingly Captain Kirk (William Shatner).

that has "many names but one promise," and which offers healing. This again is very true to the original stories, which hold out the promise of healing to all who come into its presence.

Several other episodes of the series feature Arthurian themes, including "A Late Delivery from Avalon," in which Arthur does indeed return, if not in the way anyone might have expected. Other Arthurian characters whose outlines, at least, may be discerned in the series are The Lady of the Lake, Perceval, and Merlin. Looked at as a whole, *Babylon 5* represents the most extensive treatment of the Arthurian legend set in the future, though there are, of course, numerous novels which do so—mostly without great success.

A Once and Future King

The enduring fame and potency of the Arthurian tradition continues to burn with a steady flame. New theories appear at regular intervals, suggesting, for example, that the entire saga of Arthur is localized within the borders of Wales, or exploring the myths of Caucasian tribespeople from the Russian Steppes, imported into Britain by the Roman legions, who may have brought myths that fed into the native British tales of Arthur.

In America, during the office of President John Fitzgerald Kennedy, the White House became known as Camelot and Kennedy himself was identified with Arthur. While this was doubtless a piece of political opportunism, promoted by statements to the Press by the First Lady, the myth survived Kennedy's assassination, and even gave rise to a rumor that he had not died from his injuries but remained in hiding in a vegetative state—the implication being that, like Arthur, he would one day return.

From all of this we can be certain of one thing: the long story of Arthur is by no means ended. New versions of the legends continue to appear, new stories are added at an astonishing rate: no less than 78 new novels inspired by Arthurian themes appeared in 2003. Among the scholarly community debate still rages as to whether there ever *was* a man named Arthur, or whether he was truly just a myth.

Yet some still believe the old story of Arthur's return, and perhaps even if we do not want to subscribe to the idea of a physical resurrection of the Dark-Age king, one may see the immense continuing interest in the stories and visions of Arthur and his knights as a kind of return. Indeed, perhaps he never went way at all. A quotation from the medieval *Didot Perceval* seems to sum it up:

> *Arthur had himself born to Avalon and he told his people that they should await for him and he would return. And the Britons came back to Carduel and waited for him more than forty years before they would take a king, for they believed always he would return. But this you may know in truth that some have since then seen him hunting in the forest, and they have heard his dogs with him, and some have hoped for a long time that he will return.*

APPENDIX 1

Major Sources of The Arthurian Legend

The following is a list of the major medieval texts relating to the Arthurian legends in approximate chronological order. Where no author is given, the work should be considered anonymous or traditional.

De Excidio et Conquestu Britanniae, Gildas	c. 540
Historia Britonum, Nennius	ninth century
Annales Cambriae	ninth century
Spoils of *Annwn*	ninth century
Culhwch and Olwen	eleventh century
Historia Regum Britanniae, Geoffrey of Monmouth	c. 1136
Roman de Brut, Wace	1155
Erec and Enide, Chrétien de Troyes	c. 1170
Lancelot, Chrétien de Troyes	c. 1177–81
Yvain, Chrétien de Troyes	c. 1177–81
Perceval, Chrétien de Troyes	c. 1181–90
First continuation of *Perceval*	c. 1190
Joseph of Arimathea, Robert de Boron	c. 1202
Brut, Layamon	c. 1205
Perlesvaus	c. 1208
Didot Perceval	c. 1210
Parzifal, Wolfram von Eschenbach	c. 1210
Vulgate Cycle, The	c. 1215–35
Second continuation of *Perceval*	c. 1220
Third continuation of *Perceval*	c. 1220
Diu Crone, Heinrich von dem Turlin	c. 1230
Peredur	c. 1240
Prose *Tristan*	c. 1255
Der Jungere Titural, Albrecht von Scharfenburg	c. 1274
Perceforest	c. 1335
Sone de Nansai	c. 1350
Alliterative *Morte Arthure*	c. 1390
Stanzaic *Le Morte Arthure*	c. 1400
Sir Gawain and the Green Knight	c. 1400
Le Morte d'Arthur, Sir Thomas Malory	1485

APPENDIX 2:

Warriors, Courtiers and Women of King Arthur's Court

The following list is compiled from original sources, including *Culhwch and Olwen, The Dream of Rhonabwy, The Twenty-Four Knights of Arthur's Court, The Welsh Triads* and *Welsh Genealogical Tracts.*

Names indicated with an asterisk (*) are known historical personages. Where known, the meaning of names or epithets are given in brackets after the name. The term *ap* means "son of"; *ferch* means "daughter of." Although this may seem to be no more than an incomprehensible list of unpronounceable names, these were the original heroes of the Arthurian realm, whose deeds inspired those of the literary tales.

The Men of the Court

1. Cei; 2. Bedwyr; 3. Greidawl Gallddofydd (Tamer of Enemies); 4. Gwythyr ap Greidawl; 5. Greid ap Eri; 6. Cynddylig Cyfarwydd (the Guide); 7. Tathal Twyll Golau (the Deceitful); 8. Maelwys ap Baeddan; 9. Cynchwr ap Nes; 10. Cubert ap Daere (the Irishman—possibly Curoi mac Daire); 11. Fercos ap Roch (possibly Fergus mac Roth); 12. Lluber Beuthach; 13. Corfil Berfach; 14. Gwyn ap Esni; 15. Gwyn ap Nwyfre; 16. Edern ap Nudd; 17. Cadwy ap Geraint*; 18. Fflewdur Flam Wledig (the Blazing Lord); 19. Rhuawn Bebyr ap Dorath; 20. Bradwen ap Moren Mynawg; 21. Moren Mynawg; 22. Dallaf ap Cimin ap Alun Dyfed ap Saidi ap Gwrion; 23. Uchdryd Ardwyad Cad (Protector in Battle); 24. Cynwas Cwryfagyl (the Clumsy); 25. Gwrhyr Gwarthegfras (Rich in Cattle); 26. Isberyr Ewingath (Cat Claws); 27. Galloch Gofyniad (the Hewer); 28. Duach ap Gwawrddur (the Hunchback); 29. Brath ap Gwawrddur; 30. Nerthach ap Gwawrddur; 31. Cilydd Canastyr (100 Grips); 32. Canastyr Canllaw (100 Hands); 33. Cors Cant Ewin (100 Claws); 34. Esgeir Gulhwch Gefyncawn (the Reed-cutter); 35. Dwrst Dwnhaeadn (Iron-Fist); 36. Glewlwyd Gafae Ifawr (Mighty-Grasp); 37. Llwch Llenlleawg (Mighty-Hand); 38. Anwas Adeiniawg (the Winged); 39. Sinnoch ap Seitfed ap Bedyn; 40. Wadu ap Seitfed ap Bedyn; 41. Naw ap Seitfed ap Bedyn; 42. Gwenwynwyn ap Seitfed ap Bedyn; 43. Maelap Roycol; 44. Garwyli ap Gwythawg Gwyr; 45. Gwythawg Gwyr; 46. Gormant ap Ricca; 47. Selyf ap Sinoid; 48. Gusg ap Achen; 49. Drudwas ap Tryffin; 50. Twyrch ap Peryf, 51. Twyrch ap

Anwas; 52. Sel ap Selgi; 53. Teregud ap Iaen of Caer Dathal; 54. Sulien ap Iaen of Caer Dathal; 55. Siawn ap Iaen of Caer Dathal; 56. Cradawg ap laen of Caer Dathal; 57. Mabsan ap Caw; 58. Angawddm Gofan; 59. Gwynad ap Caw; 60. Llwybyr Coch; 61. Cynwal ap Caw*; 62. Gildas ap Caw*; 63. Calchaf ap Caw*; 64. Hueil ap Caw*; 65. Samson Finsych (Dry Lips); 66. Llary ap Easnar Wledig; 67. Sarannon ap Glythfur; 68. Anynnawg ap Menw ap Teirgwaedd; 69. Fflan ap Nwyfre; 70. Geraint ap Erbin*; 71. Ermid ap Erbin; 72. Dywel ap Erbin; 73. Llawr ap Ermid; 74. Cyndrwyn ap Ermid; 75. Hafaidd Unllen (One Mantle); 76. Eiddon Fawr-frydig (the Magnanimous); 77. Rheiddon Arwy; 78. Llawrodded Farfawg (the Bearded); 79. Noddawl farf Trwch (Boar's Beard); 80. Berth ap Cado; 81. Rheiddwn ap Banon; 82. Isgofan Hael (the Generous); 83. Isgawyn ap Banon; 84. Morfran ap Tegid (the Ugly); 85. Sandaff Pryd Angel (Bright Angel); 86. Sgilti Yscawndroed (Lightfoot); 87. Henwas Adeiniawg ap Erim; 88. Carnedyr ap Gofynion Hen (the Aged); 89. Gwenwynwyn ap Naw (Arthur's Champion in Culhwch); 90. Culfanawyd ap Gwrion; 91. Dyfhwal Moel (the Bald); 92. Terynon Twrf Liant; 93. Gwrddyal ap Efrei; 94. Morgant Hael (the Generous); 95. Gwystl ap Nwython; 96. Rhun ap Nwython; 97. Llwydel ap Nwython; 98. Gwydre ap Llwydeu; 99. Eidoel ap Ner; 100. Cynyr Ceinfarfalig (Fair Beard); 101. Berwyn ap Cyrenyr; 102. Gwyddawg ap Menestyr; 103. Garanwen ap Cei; 104. Llwyd ap Cil Coed; 105. Huabwy ap Gwryon; 106. Gwyn Eddyfron; 107. Gweir ap Galellin Tal Ariant (Silver Brow); 108. Gweir Gwryhyd Enwir (Malicious in Battle); 109. Gweir Gwyn Paladr (Bright Spear); 110. Cas ap Saidi; 111. Gwrfan Arf Wyn (Wild Hair); 112. Garselit the Irishman; 113. Penawr Penbagad (Leader of the Host); 114. Atlandor ap Naw; 115. Gwyn Hywar (Steward of Cornwall); 116. Gilla Goeshydd (Stag-Shank); 117. Huarwar ap Halwn (the Unsmiling); 118. Gwarae Gwallt Eurin (Golden Hair); 119. Gwelfyl ap Gwastad; 120. Uchdryd (Cross Beard); 121. Elidyr Cyfarwydd (the Guide); 122. Brys ap Brysethach; 123. Gruddlwyn Gor (the Dwarf); 124. Eheubryd ap Cyfwlch; 125. Gorasgwrn ap Nerth; 126. Gwaeddan ap Cynfeln; 127. Dwn Diysig Unben (Valorous Chieftain); 128. Eilader ap Pen Llarcan; 129. Cynedyr Wyllt (the Wild); 130. Sawyl pen Uched (the Overlord); 131. Gwalchmai ap Gwyar (Arthur's Nephew); 132. Gwalhafad ap Gwyar; 133. Gwrhyr Gwastrad Ieithoedd (Interpreter of Tongues); 134. Iddawc Cordd Prydain (Churn of Britain); 135. Eliwod ap Madoc ap Uthyr; 136. Gwarthegyd ap Caw*; 137. Ephin ap Gwyddno*; 138. Afaon ap Taliesin; 139. Caradawg Freichfras (Strong Arm); 140. March ap Meirchyawn* (First Cousin of Arthur); 141. Cadwr* (Earl of Cornwall); 142. Urien ap Kynfarch*; 143. Owein ap Urien*; 144. Selyn ap Cynan Garwyn (White Shank); 145. Gwgawn Greddyrudd* (Red Sword); 146. Gwres ap Rheged (the Standard Bearer); 147. Blathaon ap Mwrheth; 148. Gwenloynwyri ap Naw; 149. Daned ap Ath; 150. Goreu ap Custennin (Constantine); 151. Peredur Paladyr Hir (Long Spear); 152. Nerth ap Cadarn; 153. Gweir ap Gwestyl; 154. Gadwy ap Geraint; 155. Trystan ap Talwch*; 156. Moryen Menawc (the Noble); 157. Granwen ap Llyr; 158. Llacheu ap Arthur (Son of Arthur); 159. Amr ap Arthur (Son of Arthur); 160. Cydfan ap Arthur (Son of Arthur); 161. Archfedd ap Arthur (Son of Arthur); 162. Llawfrodedd Farfawc (the Bearded); 163. Rhyawd ap Morgant; 164. Dyfyr ap Alun Dyfed; 165. Llara ap Casnir Wleddig (the Mighty); 166. Pasgen ap Urien*; 167. Gilbert ap Cadgyffro (Battle-tumult); 168. Menw ap Teirgwaedd; 169. Gwrthmwl Wledig; 170. Cawrdaf ap Caradawg Freitchfras; 171. Cadynaith ap Saidi; 172. Rhun ap Maelgwyn Gwynedd.

Advisors and Courtiers

173. Dawweir Dallben (the Blind); 174. Taliesin pen Berydd (Chief Poet); 175. Teithi Hen (the Old) ap Gwynnan; 176. Gwrfoddw Hen (the Old) (Arthur's Uncle in *Culhwch*); 177. Tegfan Gloff (the Lame); 178. Tegyr Talgellawg (the Cup Bearer); 179. Gwewlyuddyn Saer (the builder who made Arthur's Hall Ehangwen ["Fair and Roomy"]); 180. Amren ap Bedwyr (Arthur's Huntsman); 181. Rhun Rhuddwern (Red Alder) (Arthur's Huntsman); 182. Eli (Arthur's Huntsman); 183. Myr (Arthur's Huntsman); 184. Rheu Thwydd Dyrys (Fast and Cunning) (Arthur's Huntsman); 185. Trachmyr (Arthur's Huntsman); 186. Gweir Dathar Gweinidog (Arthur's Servant); 187. Eirynwych Amheibyn (the Splendid) (Arthur's Servant); 188. Cacamwri (the Thresher) (Arthur's Servant); 189. Bedwini (the Bishop); 190. Cetlirwin (the Priest).

The Women of the Court

191. Gwenhwyfar (the Queen); 192. Gwenhwyach (her Sister); 193. Rathyen ferch Clemenyl; 194. Celemon ferch Cei; 195. Tangwen ferch Gweir Dathar Gweinidog; 196. Gwen Alarch (Swan White); 197. Eurneid ferch Clydno Eidin; 198. Eneuawg ferch Bedwr; 199. Enrhydred ferch Tuduathar; 200. Gwenwledyr ferch Gwaredur Cyrfach; 201. Erdudfyl ferch Tryffin; 202. Eurolwyn ferch Gwdolyn Gor; 203. Teleri ferch Peul; 204. Indeg ferch Garwy Hir; 205. Morfudd ferch Urien Rheged*; 206. Gwelliant the Fair; 207. Creiddylad ferch Llud Llaw Ereint; 208. Ellylw ferch Noel Cyncroc; 209. Essyllt Fynwen (White Neck); 210. Essyllt Fyngul (Slender Neck).

ARTHURIAN CHARACTERS MENTIONED IN THIS BOOK

AGRAVAIN. Son of **Lot of Orkney** and **Morgause**, brother of **Gawain**, **Gaheries** and **Gareth**. Less likeable than his siblings, Agravain is involved in the plot against **Lancelot** that brings down the Round Table. He meets his death at the hands of Lancelot while fighting outside **Guinevere**'s chamber.

AMBROSIUS AURELIANUS. Successor to **Vortigern** and brother of **Uther Pendragon**.

ARTHUR. Son of **Uther** and **Igrain**. Some sources claim that his mother was among those who escaped from Atlantis before the great continent sank. Others maintain that she possessed fairy blood. Certainly Uther inherits the ancient blood of the British kings, and is descended from a line of rulers. **Merlin** brings about Arthur's birth by disguising Uther to look like Igrain's husband **Gorlois**. Arthur becomes the sacred King of Britain on drawing a sword from a stone, not Excalibur as is sometimes believed, but a symbol of his right to rule arranged by Merlin, who becomes his advisor.

BEDEVERE. One of the first to join the Fellowship of the Round Table, he is the butler to the court, organizing feasts and tournaments along with the irascible **Kay**. A warrior in his own right, Bedevere is with Arthur to the end of his life and throws the enchanted sword, Excalibur, back into the lake from which it came.

BERTILAK. Knight transformed by **Morgan** into the Green Knight. He represents winter, and is, in his alternate guise, a vegetation god whose task it is to test and initiate **Gawain** into the mysteries of the Goddess. Lady Bertilak, his wife, is forced to attempt the seduction of Gawain so that he will betray the vows of chivalry and thus damage the reputation of the Round Table. At a deeper level she is one of the aspects of the Celtic Goddess, whose role as a temptress was also designed to initiate Gawain into her service.

BORS. Cousin of **Lancelot**. One of the strongest Knights of the Round Table he is the third of the trio of successful Grail knights. Steadiness and dependability are his chief aspects. He alone returns to Camelot at the end of the Grail Quest to tell **Arthur** and his court what has occurred. Later he refuses to defend **Guinevere** against accusations of adultery, changes his mind and is relieved by Lancelot, who appears at the last moment to save her from death. Surviving most of the Fellowship, he dies in Palestine fighting in the Crusades.

BRAN. Ancestral King of Britain and one of the powerful titanic gods who ruled the land before the coming of **Arthur**. He also prefigures the Wounded/Maimed King of the later stories. At his death he commands that his head is cut off and carried to the island of Gwales where it continues to speak for many years until one of those who had accompanied it opens a forbidden door, at which point the head falls silent and begins to decay. It is then carried to the White Mount in London and buried in accordance with Bran's wishes, so that he might continue to defend the country against invasion. Arthur later orders the head dug up so that he alone is the defender of Britain.

BRANGAINE. The companion of **Isolde of Cornwall**. She gives **Tristan** and her mistress the love potion brewed by Isolde's mother, which is intended for the wedding night of Isolde with **Mark**. After Tristan becomes Isolde's lover Brangaine agrees to substitute herself on the wedding night so that Mark will not discover that Isolde is no longer a virgin.

BRISEN. The nurse of **Elaine of Corbenic** who arranges the deception by which **Galahad** is engendered, drugging **Lancelot** and causing him to believe he is bedding **Guinevere**. On waking to discover that it is Elaine beside him, Lancelot almost kills her, then becomes mad for a time. Elaine brings up Galahad before sending him to the care of nuns at Amesbury, Wiltshire

CULHWCH. Early Celtic hero whose quest for Olwen White-Footprint, daughter of Yspadadden Chief-Giant, leads him to request aid from his cousin Arthur. A fantastic collection of heroes with otherworldly abilities are dispatched to help the youth, and a mass of fragmentary hero tales are drawn upon for the adventures that follow.

DINDRAINE. The sister of **Perceval**, who accompanies the Grail knights and eventually sacrifices herself in order to heal a leprous woman. Her body is carried in the Ship of Solomon to the sacred city of Sarras, where it is buried alongside that of **Galahad**. As the only woman involved in the Grail Quest her role is of the utmost importance. She represents, along with **Elaine of Corbenic**, the feminine mysteries of the Grail.

ECTOR. The foster father of **Arthur**. He raises the young king, keeping him ignorant of his identity after being entrusted with the child by **Merlin**.

ELAINE OF ASTOLAT. The maiden by whose father **Lancelot** is secretly armed for a tournament. She falls in love with the famous knight and when she realizes that he will never return that love, she starves herself to death. Her body is put into a boat and carried down river to Camelot where all are saddened by her fate.

ELAINE OF CORBENIC. The daughter of **Pelles**, of the Grail family. She discovers and heals **Lancelot** after his spell of madness. Elaine fades rather from the scene at this juncture, although she features as the Grail Princess in some versions of the Arthurian sagas.

GAHERIES. Second son of **Lot** and **Morgause**. He discovers that his mother has taken the knight **Lamorack** as her lover, and finding them in bed together cuts off his mother's head in a fit of passion. He later dies at **Lancelot**'s hands in the battle to rescue **Guinevere** from the stake.

GALAHAD. Son of **Elaine of Corbenic** and **Lancelot**. He surpasses his father in both chivalry and purity of life, becoming the achiever of the Grail along with **Perceval** and **Bors**. His relationship with his father is touching and enlightening, and his last words are to tell Bors to "remember me to my father Sir Lancelot."

GARETH OF ORKNEY. Third son of **Lot** and **Morgause**. He comes anonymously to court and is called Beaumains (Fair Hands) by **Kay**, who puts him to work in the kitchens. He requests that he be allowed to go on the adventure of **Lynette** and distinguishes himself greatly, fighting a series of multicolored knights. He is knighted by **Lancelot** whose devoted follower he becomes, however, he and his brothers are tragically slain by his mentor during the battle to rescue **Guinevere**.

GAWAIN. Eldest son of **Lot** and **Morgause**. He is the greatest knight at the Arthurian court until the arrival of **Lancelot**. His reputation suffers due to his allegiance to the Goddess, whose champion and lover he becomes after the initiation tests of the Green Knight, and his marriage to **Ragnall**. The death of his brothers at Lancelot's hands drives him to become the bitterest foe of his once greatest friend. He dies at last, from wounds received in a fight that Lancelot never wished for. His ghost appears to **Arthur** before the battle of Camlan.

GORLOIS, DUKE OF CORNWALL. First husband of **Igrain**. He fights a bitter war with **Uther** and is finally slain at the castle of Tintagel. **Merlin** disguises Uther so that he resembles Gorlois, in which form he engenders **Arthur** upon Igrain, whom he later marries.

GROMER SOMER JOURE. Brother of **Ragnall** who challenges **Arthur** with a riddle: "What is it women most desire?" A powerful otherworldly figure and enchanter, he is defeated by Arthur with the help of **Gawain** and confesses that he was enchanted by **Morgan le Fay**.

GUINEVERE (GWENHYWFAR). Daughter of **Leodegrance**, wife of **Arthur**. Her affair with **Lancelot** destroys the kingdom, and she ends her days in the monastery of Amesbury, where she is finally buried after taking a last leave of Lancelot. Her original role in the legends was as the Flower Bride, an ancient aspect of the Goddess whose function was to be fought over by the contending powers of summer and winter. At one time the characters of Arthur and Lancelot must have taken these roles.

IGRAIN (YGAERNE). Mother of **Arthur**. Tradition speaks of her as coming from Atlantis, but in most versions of the story she is the wife of **Gorlois of Cornwall**, with whom **Uther** falls in love. Through **Merlin**'s enchantment Uther assumes the likeness of Igrain's husband so that he can beget Arthur upon her.

ISOLDE (ISOLT, ISEULT) OF CORNWALL. Daughter of King Anguish of Ireland. She is the intended wife of **Mark of Cornwall**, but becomes the lover of **Tristan**, after drinking a love potion intended for her wedding night. A famous beauty, her affair with Tristan shocks the Arthurian court and draws attention from the love of **Lancelot** and **Guinevere**. Arriving too late to save Tristan from a poisoned wound she dies and is buried alongside him in Brittany.

ISOLDE (ISOLT, ISEULT) OF THE WHITE HANDS. Daughter of the King of Brittany, she becomes **Tristan**'s wife at the behest of her brother Kaherdin. The marriage is not consummated and Isolde becomes bitter toward her husband—finally bringing about his death by lying about the color of the sails on the ship bringing **Isolde of Cornwall** to his aid. She commits suicide shortly after.

JOSEPH OF ARIMATHEA, ST. A rich Jew, with connections in the Cornish tin trade, he may have visited Britain with the young Jesus. Later, after the Crucifixion, he claims the body of the Messiah and inters it in his own tomb. As a reward he is given custody of the Grail and founds a family of guardians who watch over it until the quest of **Galahad**, a direct descendent of Joseph, is complete. He is also credited with building the first Christian church, dedicated to the Virgin Mary, at Glastonbury in Somerset.

KAY (CEI). Arthur's foster brother, and son of **Ector**. He becomes Arthur's Seneschal, and serves him faithfully in this office until the end of the Round Table. His irascible nature and occasional cruelty earn him an unsympathetic reputation, but he is a good knight for all that and seems to genuinely love Arthur.

LAMORACK. Son of **Pellinore**. One of the strongest Knights of the Round Table, he falls in love with **Morgause** and is murdered by **Gawain** and his brothers.

LANCELOT. Son of King Ban of Benwick. Sometimes called Lancelot du Lac, after his adoption in the otherworldly realm of the Lake of the Lake, he retains many qualities of the fairy knight, which enable him to take his place as the most renowned of **Arthur**'s knights. He takes over from **Gawain** the role of queen's champion, and falls in love with **Guinevere**. There are many stories that tell of Lancelot's prowess and his attempts to rid the kingdom of evil custom: in his guardianship of the land, he takes on the kingly role of Arthur. After being tricked into sleeping with **Elaine of Corbenic** Lancelot becomes mad. Elaine heals him and he becomes a part of the Grail quest. Unable to attain the vessel himself, due to his adulterous love of Guinevere, he is nonetheless represented and surpassed by **Galahad** his son. Eventually banished from court, he becomes a hermit after Arthur's passing.

LOT. King of Orkney and husband of **Morgause**. At the beginning of **Arthur**'s reign, he is one of the rebel kings. The Orkney clan, consisting of his sons **Gawain**, **Agravain**, **Gaheries** and **Gareth** and their mother, retain some animosity toward Arthur's reign; though, ironically, it is in **Mordred**, the son of Morgause by Arthur, that the seeds of rebellion surface. Lot is killed by **Pellinore**.

LYNETTE (LINET). Sometimes called *Le Demoiselle Sauvage*, Lynette comes to court asking help for her imprisoned sister, **Lyonors**. The only available knight is the recently knighted Beaumains—**Gareth**—whose inexperience she taunts unmercifully. She also appears in some stories as the guide and protector of **Owein**.

LYONORS (LIONORS). Sister of **Lynette**. She is rescued by **Gareth** who later marries her.

MARK. King of Cornwall and uncle of **Tristan**, whom he sends to obtain his bride, **Isolde**, daughter of the King of Ireland, with disastrous results for his own happiness. Isolde avoids her own wedding night by sending her companion, **Brangaine**, to Mark's bed. Mark is represented as a cuckold who condones Isolde's infidelity, though he frequently pursued the queen and his nephew.

MERLIN (MYRDDIN). Magician and guardian of the Pendragon line. Born to a virgin who was visited by a spirit, Merlin Emrys is discovered by **Vortigern**'s men as the perfect sacrifice to help seal the foundations of his tumbling-down tower. Merlin tells of the eternal battle between the dragons that lie beneath the foundations in a story that reflects the racial divisions of the time. He makes prophecies about Britain in gnomic verses and becomes the advisor of **Ambrosius Aurelianus** and his brother **Uther**, in the course of whose reign he magically builds Stonehenge. **Arthur** inherits Merlin as magical adviser for a short while, following which, according to some sources, Merlin returns to his father's realm to become the eternal guardian of Britain, or succumbs to the charms of **Nimue**, according to some French sources. Merlin is the chief architect of the Pendragon strategy and the inner guardian of the land which, in early times, was called *Clas Merddin* (Merlin's Enclosure).

MORDRED. The incestuously begotten son of **Arthur** and **Morgause**. When Arthur realizes that he has slept with his half-sister, he attempts to kill his son by issuing a Herod-like proclamation that all babies born at that time be exposed in an open boat. Mordred survives to be raised by Morgause who eventually sends him to court, though Mordred is never openly recognized as Arthur's son or successor. When the Round Table is in collapse, Mordred capitalizes on the weakness of the realm and Arthur's absence, to seize command. He is slain by Arthur, whom he mortally wounds.

MORGAN LE FAY. Daughter of **Gorlois** and **Igrain**. She is sent to a monastery ostensibly to be educated as a nun, though she learns the magical arts. She makes a political match with **Uriens of Gore** and becomes the mother of **Owein**. Ever at enmity with Arthur and his plans, she seems to be constantly plotting some new enormity. However, Morgan's role as protector of the land leads her to adopt some challenging measures to keep Arthur's kingship bright. Morgan has many early and Celtic correlatives that make plain the nature of her role as guardian of Britain's sovereignty, which she in many ways, embodies.

MORGAUSE. Wife of Lot, daughter of **Igrain** and **Gorlois**, she is married to **Lot** of Orkney, by whom she had **Gawain**,

Gaheries, **Agravain** and **Gareth**. She bears **Mordred** to Arthur, having seduced her half-brother on the eve of his coronation. She becomes **Lamorack**'s mistress and, on being discovered in bed with him, is slain by **Gaheries**.

NIMUE (NINIANE, VIVIENNE). The daughter of Dionas, a gentleman who was a votary of Diana, Nimue is conflated with the Lady of the Lake in later traditions. **Merlin** teaches her magic, and eventually becomes infatuated with her, according to Malory, so that she is able to entice and imprison him under a great stone. She then adopts Merlin's magical mantle throughout the rest of the tales.

OWEIN (YWAIN). Son of **Morgan** and **Uriens**, he is one of the earliest Arthurian knights and, in *The Mabinogion*, becomes the husband of the Lady of the Fountain and the master of the Enchanted Games. In later traditions, Owein prevents Morgan from killing his father. He also rescues a lion that becomes his companion, and so is sometimes called the Knight of the Lion.

PALOMIDES. Saracen knight, in love with **Isolde of Cornwall**. He becomes the pursuer of the Questing Beast, after the death of **Pellinore**.

PELLES (PELLEAM, PELLAM). King of Corbenic, of the Grail family, Pelles is wounded with the Dolorous Spear by Balin and so becomes the King of the Waste Land (also known, depending on the source, as the Maimed, Wounded, or Fisher King). His lands can only be restored by the Grail winner. Pelles condones the use of magic to lure **Lancelot** to sleep with his daughter, **Elaine**, in order that the achiever of the Grail can be engendered.

PELLINORE. Father of **Perceval** and **Lamorack**. His chief task is the pursuit of the Questing Beast. Because Pellinore kills **Lot**, there is a long and bitter feud between his family and the Orkney clan. Eventually **Gawain** and **Gaheries** slay Pellinore in revenge.

PERCEVAL. Son of **Pellinore**, and one of the Grail winners. According to most traditions, Perceval is raised by his mother in ignorance of arms and courtesy, but his natural prowess leads him to Arthur's court where he immediately sets off in pursuit of a knight who has insulted **Guinevere**. His further training in arms brings him into the hall of the Fisher/Wounded King where he neglects to ask the all-healing "Grail Question" out of ill-placed courtesy. His subsequent quest and discovery of the Grail is related in the earlier traditions, where he becomes the new Grail guardian. However, later texts replace Perceval with **Galahad** as the Grail winner. Perceval then becomes Galahad's companion. Perceval's early ignorance has tagged him "the Perfect Fool," but his is a Christ-like simplicity without offense which matures into real insight and wisdom.

RAGNALL. Sister of **Gromer**, she is enchanted into the shape of an ugly hag by **Morgan**, and comes to the rescue of Arthur who strives to find the answer to Gromer's riddle. She agrees to tell him the answer in return for her marriage to **Gawain**. Arthur accepts on Gawain's behalf. Gromer arrives and poses the question: "What is it women most desire?," to which Arthur relates the answer: "Women desire to have sovereignty over men." Gawain and Ragnall are wed and, at their first kiss, she is transformed into a beautiful maiden. However, Gawain is asked to decide whether she shall be fair by day and foul by night, or the reverse. Fully realizing the meaning of the riddle, Gawain begs her to chose and Ragnall is released from her spell.

TRISTAN (TRISTRAM). **Mark**'s nephew, lover of **Isolde of Cornwall**. Sent by Mark to fetch his bride, Tristan falls in love with Isolde by means of a love potion. Their checkered love is marked by continual pursuits by Mark, near escapes and subterfuge. After being healed of a poisoned arrow wound by another Isolde (of Brittany), Tristan marries her, but is unable to find happiness. Tristan dies without seeing the former Isolde. He is the truly bardic knight, without the pristine chivalry of **Lancelot**: a true Celt in his poetic lovemaking.

URIENS OF GORE. Father of **Owein** and husband of **Morgan**. Uriens is one of the early rebels against **Arthur**, but he becomes one of his most faithful followers.

UTHER PENDRAGON. Father of **Arthur**, second husband of **Igrain**. Uther sees Igrain and lusts for her. He lays siege to her husband, **Gorlois**'s, castle and, in his absence, and with the aid of **Merlin**, takes on the shape of his rival in order to sleep with her. In the same hour Gorlois perishes in battle. Uther retains the earliest resonance of the Arthurian legend, the bedrock upon which they are established; his taking of Igrain for himself reveals him to have practiced "the Custom of the Pendragon"—a form of *droit du seigneur* with the women of his realm.

VORTIGERN. The predecessor of **Ambrosius**, who invites Saxon mercenaries into Britain in order to protect the realm: an action hardly popular among the people. His attempts to build a stronghold came to nothing, for it keeps tumbling down. Counseled by his druids to sacrifice a boy without a father, Vortigern finds **Merlin** who prophesies the fate of Britain. Vortigern dies shortly after.

GLOSSARY

apportion To distribute divided amounts of something, such as land.
Arthurian Relating to King Arthur in some way.
chivalry The formal customs of medieval knighthood.
deity A god or goddess.
endeavor A goal that one attempts to achieve.
enmity Ill will between two or more people or groups.
Excalibur The sword that King Arthur used.
Guinevere King Arthur's wife and Lancelot's mistress.
medieval Having to do with the Middle Ages.
mythic Of or relating to legend or fantasy.
pagan A person with no religious or moral affiliations.
penance The act of expressing sorrow for one's sinful deeds.
primitive Of or relating to an early time in development.
prophecy A prediction or foretelling.
protagonist The main character in a literary work.
Round Table The large table of King Arthur and his knights.
scabbardless Without a sheath for a sword.

FOR FURTHER READING

This is only a selection from the vast range of Arthurian fiction and poetry that has appeared over the last 50 years and which continues to appear on an almost monthly basis.

Eliot, T.S., *The Waste Land & Other Poems*, Faber and Faber, London, 1971

Heath-Stubbs, J., *Artorius*, Enitharmon Press, London, 1974

Holdstock, R., *Celtika, The Merlin Codex 1*, Simon & Schuster, London, 2000

Jones, D., *The Sleeping Lord*, Faber and Faber, London, 1974

Matthews, John, *The Song of Arthur*, Quest Books, Wheaton, Illinois, 2002

Matthews, John, *The Song of Taliesin*, Quest Books, Wheaton, Illinois, 2001

Paxson, D. L., *The Hallowed Isle* (Books 1–4), Avon Books, New York, 1999–2000

Paxson, D. L., *The White Raven*, William Morrow, New York, 1988

Williams, C., *War in Heaven*, Faber & Faber, London, 1947

FOR MORE INFORMATION

Arthuriana (Quarterly Journal for the International Arthurian Society—North American Branch. Dedicated to studies of all aspects of the Arthurian story from Middle Ages to the present. Write to: Box 750432, Southern Methodist University, Dallas Texas 75275-0432, USA.

Pendragon Journal of the Pendragon Society (Quarterly British Journal for all those interested in Arthurian matters). Write to: Simon & Anne Rouse, 7 Verlon Close, Montgomery, Powys SY15 6SH, UK.

The International Arthurian Society (The main Arthurian society in the world to which all Arthurian scholars subscribe. It holds a biennial conference and produces a bibliographical bulletin every year.) British Branch write to: Secretary/Treasurer: Dr. Francois Le Saux, Dept of French Studies, University of Reading, Reading, RG6 2AA, UK.

North American Branch, write to: Professor Jean Blacker, Dept of Modern Foreign Languages and Literatures, Kenyon College, Gambier, OH 43022, USA.

Web Sites

Due to the changing nature of Internet links, Rosen Publishing has developed an online list of Web sites related to the subject of this book. This site is updated regularly. Please use this link to access the list:

http://www.rosenlinks.com/pth/kiar

JOHN & CAITLÎN MATTHEWS have a Web site giving details of forthcoming books, events and courses in their quarterly online newsletter, *Hallowquest*. See www.hallowquest.org.uk. If you wish to receive the newsletter by mail, send £8 (in UK) or £16 (outside UK) as a sterling check payable to Caitlîn Matthews, or US $25 in cash to Hallowquest Newsletter, BCM Hallowquest, London WC1N 3XX, UK.

BIBLIOGRAPHY

Angebert, Jean-Michel, *The Occult & the Third Reich*, Macmillan, New York, 1974

The Arthurian Book of Days, Sidgwick & Jackson, London, St Martin's Press, New York, 1990

An Arthurian Reader, Aquarian Press, Wellingborough, Northamptonshire, 1988

The Arthurian Tarot: A Hallowquest, Aquarian Press, Wellingborough, Northamptonshire, 1990

Ashe, G., "Merlin in the Earliest Records" in *The Book of Merlin*, Ed. R.J. Stewart. Blandford Press, Poole, Dorset, 1987.

At the Table of the Grail, Watkins Publishing, London, 2002

Baigent, Michael, Richard Leigh and Henry Lincoln, *Holy Blood, Holy Grail*, Jonathan Cape, London, 1986

Barron, W. R. J., Ed., *The Arthur of the English*, University of Wales Press, Cardiff, 2001

Bede, *A History of the English Church and People*, Penguin Books, London, 1955

Bernard of Clairvaux, *Treatise in Praise of the New Order of Knighthood*, Cistercian Publishing, New Jersey, 1976

Birks, Walter, and R. A. Gilbert, *The Treasure of Montségur*, Cruicible, London, 1987

Blake, Steve, and Scott Lloyd, *The Keys to Avalon: The True Location of Arthur's Kingdom Revealed*, Element Books, Shaftesbury, Dorset, 2000

Blake, Steve, and Scott Lloyd, *Pendragon: the Definitive Account of the Origins of Arthur*, Rider, London, 2002

The Book of Arthur: Lost Tales from the Round Table, Vega, London, 2002

Bradley, Marion Zimmer, *The Mists of Avalon*, Michael Joseph, London, 1983

Bradley, Michael with Deanna Theilman-Bean, *The Holy Grail Across the Atlantic*, Hounslow Press, Toronto, 1989

Bradshaw, G., *Down the Long Wind*, Methuen, London, 1988

Brengle, Richard L. Ed., *Arthur King of Britain*, Prentice-Hall, New Jersey, 1964

Bromwich, Rachel, *Triodd Ynys Prydein* (*The Welsh Triads*), University of Wales Press, Cardiff, 1977

Bromwich, Rachel, A. O. H. Jarman & B. F. Roberts, Eds., *The Arthur of the Welsh*, University of Wales Press, Cardiff, 1993

Bruce, Christopher W., *The Arthurian Name Dictionary*, Garland Publishing Inc., New York & London, 1999

Bryant, Nigel, *The High Book of the Grail: A Translation of the 13th Century Romance of Perlesvaus*, D.S. Brewer/Rowman & Littlefield, Woodbridge, Suffolk, 1978

Bryant, Nigel, *Merlin and the Grail: The Trilogy of Arthurian Romances Attributed to Robert de Boron*, D. S. Brewer, Woodbridge, Suffolk, 2001

Campbell, David E., *The Tale of Balin from the Romance of the Grail*, Northwestern University Press, 1972

Celtic Battle Heroes with Bob Stewart, Firebird Books, Poole, Dorset, 1988

A Celtic Reader, Aquarian Press, Wellingborough, Northamptonshire, 1990

Chadwick, Nora K., *The Celtic Realms*, Penguin Books, London, 1967

Chrétien de Troyes, *Arthurian Romances* [*Erec*, *Cligés*, *The Knight of the Cart, The Knight with the Lion, The Story of the Grail*], translated by William W. Kibler and Carleton W. Carroll, Penguin Books, London, 1991

Chrétien de Troyes, *Perceval, or the Story of the Grail*, translated by Nigel Bryant, D.S. Brewer, Cambridge, 1982

Churchill, Sir Winston, A *History of the English Speaking Peoples Vol 1*, Cassell Reference, London, 2002

Churchyard, Thomas, *The Worthiness of Wales*, Burt Franklin, New York, 1967

Coghlan, Ronan, *The Illustrated Encyclopedia of Arthurian Legends*, Element Books, Shaftesbury, Dorset, 1993

Comfort, William W., *The Quest of the Holy Grail*, J.M. Dent, 1926

Cooke, Brian Kennedy, *The Quest of the Beast*, Edmund Ward, London, 1957

Currer-Briggs, Noel, *The Shroud and the Grail*, Weidenfeld & Nicolson, London, 1987

De Lint, Charles, *Spiritwalk*, Ace Books, New York, 1992

Dillon, Miles, *The Cycles of the Kings*, Dent, London, 1946

Doel, Fran, and Geoff and Terry Lloyd, *Worlds of Arthur*, Tempus Publishing, Stroud, Gloucestershire, 1998

Durrell, Shelly, *Healing the Fisher King*, The Tao Press, Miami, 2002

The Elements of Celtic Tradition, Element Books, Shaftesbury, Dorset, 1989

The Elements of the Goddess, Element Books, Shaftesbury, Dorset, 1989

Eliot, T.S., *The Waste Land & Other Poems*, Faber and Faber, London, 1971

Evans, Sebastian, *In Quest of the Holy Graal*, J.M. Dent, 1898

Fionn mac Cumhail: Champion of Ireland, Firebird Books, Poole, Dorset, 1988

Fisher, Catherine, *Corbenic*, Red Fox, London, 2002

Frankland, E., *The Bear of Britain*, Macdonald, London, 1941

From the Isles of Dream, Floris Books, Edinburgh, 1993

Gawain, Knight of the Goddess, Inner Traditions, Rochester, Vermont, 2003

Geoffrey of Monmouth, *History of the Kings of Britain*, translated by Lewis Thorp, Penguin Books, London, 1966

Giles, J. A., Ed., *Six Old English Chronicles*, G. Bell & Sons, London, 1910

A Glastonbury Reader, Aquarian Press, Wellingborough, Northamptonshire, 1991

The Grail: Quest for the Eternal, Thames & Hudson, London, 1981, Crossroads, 1990

The Grail Seeker's Companion with Marian Green, Thoth Books, London, 2003

Guest, Charlotte, *The Mabinogion*, Everyman Library, 1906

Harty, Kevin J., Ed., *King Arthur on Film*, McFarland & Co. Inc., Jefferson, North Carolina, 1999

Heath-Stubbs, J., *Artorius*, Enitharmon Press, London, 1974

Higham, N. J., *King Arthur: Myth Making and History*, Routledge, London, 2002

Holdstock, R., *Celtika, The Merlin Codex 1*, Simon & Schuster, London, 2000

Holdstock, R., *The Iron Grail: The Merlin Codex 2*, Simon & Schuster, London, 2002

Hughes, Jonathan, *Arthurian Myths and Alchemy: The Kingship of Edward IV*, Tempus Publishing, Stroud, Gloucestershire, 2003

Jarman, A. O. H., *Geoffrey of Monmouth*, University of Wales Press, Cardiff, 1966

Jones, D., *The Anathemata*, Faber and Faber, London, 1952

Jones, D., *In Parenthesis*, Faber and Faber, London, 1937

Jones, D., *The Sleeping Lord*, Faber and Faber, London, 1974

Jones, Thomas, "The Black Book of Carmarthen Stanzas of the Graves" in *Proceedings of the British Academy 53*, (1967) pp. 97–137

Jung, Emma, and Marie-Louise von Franz, *The Grail Legend*, Hodder & Stoughton, London, 1971

King Arthur and the Goddess of the Land: the Divine Feminine in the Mabinogion, Inner Traditions, Rochester, Vermont, 2002

King Arthur's Britain: A Photographic Odyssey, with Michael J. Stead, Cassell, London, 1995

Lacy, Norris J. Ed., *The New Arthurian Encyclopaedia*, St James Press, Chicago & London, 1991

Lacey, Norris J., and Geoffrey Ashe, *The Arthurian Handbook*, Garland Press, New York, 1988

Lacey, Norris et al., Eds., *Lancelot–Grail: the Old French Vulgate and Post Vulgate in Translation (Vols 1–5)*, Garland Publishing, New York & London, 1993–98

Ladies of the Lake, with Caitlín Matthews, Aquarian Press, Wellingborough, Northamptonshire, 1992

Lawhead, S., *Arthur*, Lion Books, Oxford, 1989

Lawhead, S., *Merlin*, Lion Books, Oxford, 1988

Lawhead, S., *Taliesin*, Lion Books, Oxford, 1988

Layamon, *The Brut in Arthurian Chronicles*, translated by E. Mason, Everyman Library, 1962

Legendary Britain: An Illustrated Journey, with R. J. Stewart, Cassell, London, 1989

Little Book of Celtic Wisdom, with Caitlín Matthews, Element Books, Shaftesbury, Dorset, 1993

Littleton, C. Scott, and Linda Malcor, *From Scythia to Camelot*, Garland Publishing, New York & London, 1994

Loomis, R.S., *The Grail From Celtic Myth to Christian Symbol*, University of Wales Press, Cardiff, 1963

Mabon & the Guardians of Britain: Hero Myths in the Mabinogion, Inner Traditions, Rochester, Vermont, 2002

Madden, Sir Frederic, *Syr Gawayne*, AMS Press, New York, 1971

Malory, Sir Thomas, Ed. John Matthews, *Le Morte D'Arthur*, Orion, London, 2002

Marie de France, introduction by Glyn S. Burgess and Keith Busby, *The Lais Trans*, London, Penguin Books, 1986.

Markale, Jean, *King Arthur, King of Kings*, Gordon & Cremonesi, London, 1977

Masefield, John, *Arthurian Poems*, Boydell Press, Woodbridge, Suffolk, 1994

Matarasso, P. M., translator, *The Quest for the Holy Grail*, Penguin Books, London, 1969

Matthews, Caitlín, *The Celtic Book of the Dead*, Thorsons, London, 1992

Matthews, John, *The Aquarian Guide to British and Irish Mythology*, with Caitlín Matthews, Aquarian Press, Wellingborough, Northamptonshire, 1988

Matthews, John, *The Song of Arthur*, Quest Books, Wheaton, Illinois, 2002

Matthews, John, *The Song of Taliesin*, Quest Books, Wheaton, Illinois, 2001

Meeks, John, and Doris, "The Temple of the Grail" in *The Golden Blade*, Rudolf Steiner Press, 1981

Merlin Through the Ages, with R. J. Stewart, Cassell, London, 1995

"Merlin's Esplumoir" in *Merlin and Woman*, Ed., R. J. Stewart, Blandford, London, 1988

Moffat, Alistair, *Arthur and the Lost Kingdoms*, Weidenfeld & Nicolson, London, 1999

Morris, John, *The Age of Arthur London*, Weidenfeld & Nicolson, London, 1973

Morris, John, *British History and the Welsh Annals*, Phillimore, London & Chichester 1980, [Nennius and the *Annales Cambriae*]

Parry, J. J., *The Art of Courtly Love by Andreas Capellanus*, Columbia University Press, New York, 1941

Parry, J. J., *Vita Merlini*, University of Illinois, 1925

Paxson, D. L., *The Hallowed Isle* (Books 1–4), Avon Books, New York, 1999–2000

Paxson, D. L., *The White Raven*, William Morrow, New York, 1988

Poulson, Christine, *The Quest for the Grail: Arthurian Legends in British Art 1840–1920*, Manchester University Press, 1999

Powys, John Cooper, *Porius (*Complete Edition), Colgate University Press, New York, 1994

Reiss, Edmund, L.H. Reiss and B. Taylor, *Arthurian Legend and Literature: An Annotated Bibliography. Vol 1: The Middle Ages*, Garland Publishing Inc., New York & London, 1984

Reno, Frank D., *The Historic King Arthur*, McFarland & Co., Jefferson, North Carolina, 1996

Roach, William, *The Continuations of the Old French Perceval*, American Philiosophical Society, 1949–52 (3 vols), Philadelphia

Schlauch, Margaret, *Medieval Narrative: A Book of Translations*, Geordian Press, 1969

Sinclair, Andrew, *The Sword & the Grail*, Crown Publishing, 1993

Skeels, Dell, *The Romance of Perceval in Prose: A Translation of the Didot Perceval*, University of Washington Press, 1966

Skene, W. F., *The Four Ancient Books of Wales*, AMS Press, New York, 1984–85

Sklar, Elizabeth S., and D. L. Hoffman, *King Arthur in Popular Culture*, McFarland & Co. Jefferson, North Carolina, 2002

Snyder, Christopher, *An Age of Tyrants: Britain & the Britons, AD 400–600*, Sutton Publishing, Stroud, Gloucestershire, 1998

Snyder, Christopher, *Exploring the World of King Arthur*, Thames & Hudson, London, 2000

Sommer, H. Oskar, *The Vulgate Version of the Arthurian Romances*, the Carnegie Institute, Washington, 1908–16 (8 vols)

Sources of the Grail, Floris Books, Edinburgh, 1998

Stein, Walter Johannes, *The Ninth Century: World History in the Light of the Holy Grail*, with an introduction by John Matthews, Temple Lodge Press, London, 1991

Stewart, Mary, *The Crystal Cave*, Hodder & Stoughton, London, 1976

Stewart, Mary, *The Last Enchantment*, Hodder & Stoughton, London, 1979

Stewart, R. J., Ed., *The Book of Merlin*, Blandford Press, Poole, Dorset, 1987

Stewart, R. J., Ed., *Merlin and Women*, Blandford Press, Poole, Dorset, 1988

Stewart, R. J., *The Mystic Life of Merlin*, Arkana, 1986

Stewart, R. J., *The Prophetic Vision of Merlin*, Arkana, 1986

Sutcliff, R., *Sword at Sunset*, Hodder & Stoughton, London, 1963

Taliesin: the Last Celtic Shaman, with additional material by Caitlín Matthews, Inner Traditions, Rochester, Vermont, 2002

Tennyson, Alfred, *Idylls of the King*, Penguin Books, London, 1983

Thompson, A. W., *The Elucidation*, New York Institute of French Studies, 1931

Tolstoy, Nikolai, *The Coming of the King*, Bantam Press, London, 1988

Tolstoy, Nikolai, "Nennius, Chapter 56," in *Bulletin of Celtic Studies*, Vol. 19, 1961, pp. 118–62

Tolstoy, Nikolai, *The Quest For Merlin*, Hamish Hamilton, London, 1985

Treece, H., *The Great Captains*, Savoy Books, London, 1980

Von Franz, M. L., and C. G. Jung, *His Myth in Our Time*, Hodder & Stoughton, London, 1972

Wace, Geoffrey, *The Brut,* translated by E. Mason, Everyman Library, 1962

Warriors of Arthur, with Bob Stewart, Blandford Press, Poole, Dorset, 1987

Webster, K. G. T., translator, *Lanzalet of Ulrich von Zatzikhoven*, Columbia University Press, New York, 1951

Wheatley, H. B., Ed., *The English Merlin*, Early English Text Society, London, 1865–1869

Wheeler, Francis Rolt, *Mystic Gleams From the Holy Grail*, Rider & Co., *c.* 1948

White, T.H., *The Once and Future King*, Collins, London, 1958

White T.H., *The Book of Merlyn*, Collins, London, 1978

Williams, C., *Taliesin Through Logres, The Region of the Summer Stars & The Arthurian Torso*, Wm. Eerdmans, Wheaton, Illinois, 1974

Williams, C., *War in Heaven*, Faber & Faber, London, 1947

Williams, Hugh, *Two Lives of Gildas, by the Monk of Ruys and Caradoc of Llancarven*, Llanerch Enterprises, 1990

Wilson, Ian, *The Turin Shroud*, Gollancz, London, 1979

Wolfram von Eschenbach, *Parzival*, translated by A. T. Hatto, Penguin Books, London, 1980

Wolfram von Eschenbach, *Titurel*, translated by Charles E. Passage, Frederick Ungar, 1984

INDEX